CHILLING TALES FROM NOTTINGHAMSHIRE

First published in Great Britain in 2010 by
The Derby Books Publishing Company Limited
3 The Parker Centre,
Derby, DE21 4SZ.

© **Netty**, 2010

ISBN 978-1-85983-798-6

Printed and bound by Cromwell Press Group, Trowbridge, Wiltshire.

CHILLING TALES FROM
NOTTINGHAMSHIRE

PRESENT-DAY EXPERIENCES OF THE PARANORMAL

To Darcy
Enjoy the ghost walk
Lots of Love
Netty
x

NETTY

DB PUBLISHING

For Leeky, Jack,
Hannah, Olivia and Faith

CONTENTS

FOREWORD

Being Derbyshire born and bred, I knew of the rivalry between the two Midland cities of Derby and Nottingham but had never witnessed it first hand until I embarked on my book signings for *Chilling Tales from Derbyshire*.

Every time I took to my seat with my pen poised to sign a copy of my latest book, somebody in the queue would start talking about Nottinghamshire and the fact that they had more ghosts than Derby and that they could certainly give the 'ghost capital' of England a run for its money.

Most people have heard of Nottingham's 'famous' ghost stories such as 'Yorkey', the old landlord who haunts Ye Olde Trip to Jerusalem, or the cased sailing ship at the same establishment, which according to legend will kill whoever removes it from its case to clean it. Could this be simply coincidence? Or could it really be a curse? Who knows. But nobody is taking any chances as the ship has not been cleaned for over 50 years! Then there is the case of the millionaire businessman Anwar Rashid in 2008, who purchased the magnificent Clifton Hall but reportedly had to move his family out of their new home due to a series of very frightening hauntings.

I requested people's own experiences and soon the letters started pouring in, with ordinary Nottinghamshire folk reliving their paranormal stories. And so *Chilling Tales from Nottinghamshire* was born.

It would be a braver woman than I to take sides on which end of the A52 has the most ghosts, so I will leave it up to you, the reader, to make up your own mind. As the saying goes, 'May the best team win!'

THANKS

I would like to thank my wonderful husband Leeky, who has always supported me in my writing and thankfully loves me for being me! Big thanks to my wonderful children Jack, Hannah, Olivia and Faith. I would also like to thank my Mum, Dad, Heather, Andrew, Paul, Lynda, Mark, Lorraine, Lynette and Tony for always being there. My nieces and nephews, Chris, Emily and Kerris, and Joe Alexander Simpson, who moaned at me for not mentioning him in my last book! Matt and Claire, who have always been keen supporters of my writing and have provided us with a bolt hole and hot tub when we needed to escape.

Thank you also to the BBC and *Nottingham Evening Post* for all the publicity that they have given this book and finally to the people of Nottinghamshire, without whose willingness to share their stories you would be reading an empty book.

Wishing you all love, light and laughter.

Netty x

DISCLAIMER

Neither the author nor the publisher can guarantee the authenticity of the stories that have been submitted and included in this book. They have been included and accepted in good faith. The witness account of events have been published as described first hand to the author and have not been altered in any way other than for ease of understanding. The identity of the witness has been protected as requested when submitting their account for inclusion in the book.

CHAPTER 1
GHOSTS

The *Oxford English Dictionary* states that the word ghost means: *noun:* an apparition of a dead person which is believed to appear to the living.

But what *is* a ghost? If I did a national survey and asked the question, then, chances are, there would be a flurry of different answers and opinions. Most scholars, however, believe that the interpretation of what is perceived as a 'ghost' is subjective to the witnesses' own life experiences, and scientific and religious beliefs, along with their state of mind when then experience occurred.

Personally, I believe that true ghosts follow three particular traits, and I always use the same phrasing and terminology in all my books and lectures concerning this subject as a baseline for debate. They are as follows:

THE THREE TRAITS OF A TRUE GHOST

The ghost is always human, or, to be accurate in my explanation, the ghost is the disembodied conscious energy of a once living person. This means that, for whatever reason, and one we will probably never fully understand, some people when they have died leave their physical body to decay and remain in a spiritual state on the physical plane.

Many people often mistake angels and other supernatural entities as ghosts but these are celestials and have never been human and never existed in the physical state. This point is important to remember, as the very nature of the entity might allow us to shed some light on the purpose and nature of the sighting and what the entity can and cannot do with the boundaries of linear time, space and laws of physics.

The second feature of a true ghost is that the ghost is interactive to some degree. It has the ability to manipulate matter, seemingly observe their surroundings and be observed either with the naked eye or by use of electronic capturing devices. Now, before you cry out that the same could be said for spirit guides, residual entities or poltergeists, which is indeed true (especially by poltergeists), making at least some of them potentially ghosts, for the most part such apparitions are at best manifestations of conscious energy and not ghosts in their own right.

The third characteristic is unique to ghosts as they are not naturally part of the spiritual realms but beings that exist in parallel with both the spiritual and physical worlds and have influences in both.

I believe that ghosts are beings that are unnaturally confined to the physical realm for a variety of reasons, usually having to do with either a free-will decision to stay behind or an unwillingness to completely move on to their next level of existence. In essence, then, depending upon your point of view, ghosts are either 'trapped' or choose to reside in a type of 'twilight' state that exists between the spiritual and physical realms, effectively making them residents of neither the physical nor the spiritual realm.

So, now that we understand what we mean by the term 'ghost', let the Tales begin...

THE MINSTER MONK

My cousin had come down from Scotland to spend the week with us, so we planned to show her all the beautiful sights around Nottinghamshire, despite the weather being awful during her visit. On Sunday afternoon we decided to visit Southwell Minster, so that she could see for herself the Anglo-Saxon architecture that she was so fond of.

My cousin could not get over the sheer size of the Minster and was keen to explore inside. When we entered and walked down the isle my cousin whispered to me that she wanted to say a prayer for her family back in Sterling, so we quietly slid into an empty pew and sat down. Although I am not religious myself, I decided that it would not do any harm to perhaps say a few prayers for my own family, and so we both bowed our heads and lost ourselves in our silent thoughts. We must have been that way for at least five minutes before I opened my eyes and raised my head without a sound, so not to disturb my cousin who was still very much in prayer. I took the opportunity to look around the Minster from my pew and was startled when my cousin turned her head to the right and said 'Thank you'.

Curious, I asked her whom she was thanking. Surely, I thought, if she was still praying she would have been silent.

'I was thanking the monk who was sitting at the side of me and chanting as I prayed,' she replied.

'What monk?' I asked. 'There is nobody but you and I on this pew, and both the pews in front and behind are also empty.'

My cousin gave me a look and then gazed around her, and to her amazement the monk had gone – and we were indeed very much alone.

TAKE THIS AS A WARNING

When I was younger my friends and I would visit the wood yard on Ayden Road to make dens, even though it was strictly forbidden to play there due to the dangers of falling wood. Obviously, boys being boys we would always get into mischief and thought we were invincible, so of course anything we were told not to do, we would pride ourselves in doing.

On one particular day my friends and I arrived at the wood yard and started to play on the logs, which were stacked up into large piles. We were running up and down them and generally having fun, larking about and making dens and such like, when all of a sudden one of my friends froze on the spot, staring straight ahead with a look of terror on his face. Without making a sound, we all slowed to see what he was staring at, and there we saw the ghost of a small boy floating towards him. As soon as we picked up the courage we ran as fast as we could, scared out of our minds.

We later found out that in 1948–49 a young boy had been playing in the wood yard, making dens as we used to, and he had knocked one of the towering pile of logs, which fell on top of him and killed him. Could this have been the same boy, who returned to warn us of the perils?

THE ROOM WITH A VIEW

My house in Chilwell was built over three levels, with a small dining room on the second floor. The house also had cavity wall insulation and was, in my opinion, too hot most of the time, even when we had the heating switched off. It was too hot except one room, the dining room, where we could never get rid of a cold spot towards the corner of the room. The rest of the room would be warm but as you approached that corner, you immediately felt as though you had entered a freezer, yet there was no logical explanation for it.

It was really starting to annoy me and so my husband purchased an additional heater and placed it in the cold corner. Yet, even with the heater turned to full, it did nothing to elevate the cold spot.

Several months after the heater was purchased we hosted a dinner party and invited a lady from my work and her husband whom we had never met before. The evening was going well and we started to talk about a number of subjects, including the fact that my friend's husband attended a spiritualist church. No sooner had he said the words, his eyes darted to the 'cold corner' and he seemed to lose all focus, ignoring everbody in the room and just sitting there, transfixed to the corner.

My husband was interested to find out what he had been looking at, but to be honest I was too scared at the possibilities and quickly made my way into the kitchen with my friend, leaving the two men to talk. A few moments later my husband came in to us, asked for some salt and returned back to the dining room.

After what seemed like hours – but in reality could only have been about 10 minutes – the men walked into the kitchen laughing and told us that we would not have any more problems with the 'cold spot' in the future.

The rest of the night was really pleasant as we sat in the lounge and avoided the dining room, but eventually my curiosity got the better of me and I had to know what had happened in the room when I left.

My friend's husband told us he had seen that there was a ghost of a young girl curled up in the corner of the dining room, almost like she was protecting herself from a beating. Because he had some sort of Mediumship skills, she was able to communicate with him and it was established that she was unaware that she had died and was asking for her mother. He said that the two men had been able to send her to the light and described how the room went very hot and almost electrified when they felt her leave.

I did not know whether the two men were trying to scare my friend and I or if it had happened the way that they said, but all I know is that since that night we have had no more problems with cold spots in that room...

FLAMING 'ECK!

The year must have been about 1949, and my brother Stan and I were what you would term 'little buggers'! Our mother used to dress us in the same green woollen tank tops, grey shorts and brown balaclavas, and we were not allowed out without the blasted thing for fear of us catching a cold, meaning she would have had to take time off her work as a cleaner to nurse us back to health.

We lived in a terrace house in St Annes and never had a penny to our name, except the odd one, which we found near the coal yard, left when the workers had jumped off their carts and spilt their takings. Every day we would go the yard to see if Lady Luck was shining down on us, but on many occasions all we went home with was a lump of coal. We would run into the house and present our Mam with the coal, beaming from side to side like we had just given her the crown jewels. It was not enough for her to start a fire with, but in our minds we had contributed to the household and that was important, even at that young age.

It was nearing my Mam's birthday and my brother and I were desperate to get her a present, to prove that we were now grown up, even if we had a combined age of 11. So we got an old box which had coloured flowers around it, before deciding to go scrumping for apples and pears to put inside it.

We decided that we should venture further into St Annes where the bigger houses stood as we had seen an end semi with fruit trees in the garden. Upon finding the house my brother and I carefully climbed over the wooden fence and found ourselves in the longest grass that we had ever seen. We then started to make our way up the trees to collect the pears and hid them in our tank tops.

Just as we had about reached our fill, we heard a booming voice shouting at us to 'Get off the land'. Both my brother and I looked in the direction from where the voice came, both frozen up the tree with fear as we saw an old man, standing in the doorway with what looked like flames flickering all around him.

We jumped from the tree and ran all the way back home to be greeted by our Dad, who was standing in the kitchen. Seeing the fear on our faces he managed to get a confession about where we had been, but rather than being angry he was so worried about the man in the fire, that he got us to take him to the house to see if he could help.

On approaching the scene, my Dad kept asking if it was the right house as he could see by the state of it that nobody had lived in there for a long time. We took him round the back and climbed over the fence, the grass was just as we said, the fruit trees were just as we said, but the strange thing was that where the man had been standing in the doorway, there was nothing more than a boarded-up door, which could clearly not have been opened for years.

My Dad gave my brother and I the biggest hiding all the way home for telling lies and wasting his time, and our Mam never did get her fresh fruit bowl for her birthday. But even after all these years my brother and I can remember the old man in flames like it was yesterday.

ROOM FOR TWO

I loved my childhood home in Toton until one night in September 2000, when my view of it changed forever.

I was 14 and had just gone to bed. I was not yet asleep and decided to read for a bit as I was not in the least sleepy. No sooner had I turned my first page when I felt someone or something sit down on the end of the bed near my feet, and then, to my growing horror, the back of someone's hand, wet and cold to the touch, slowly started gently stroking down the right side of my face to my shoulder. I shut my eyes tight, frozen to the bed with fear. I tried to scream but no sound came out of my mouth. All of a sudden there was a big bang in the room like a door slamming hard – and immediately the weight left my feet, the mattress rose at the bottom as if someone had stood up and the cold hand against my face went away.

I ran out of the room as fast as I could, almost jumping down the stairs and into the lounge where my parents were watching TV. I asked them if they had been upstairs but they said that they had not moved and had just been sat there watching *The Bill*. I am not sure if they believed me but I insisted that I slept in their room that night, and before I went back in my own room each night, I made sure that my Dad had looked all over the room for any ghosts or monsters.

I never saw or felt anything like it before and thankfully my parents decided to move to Chilwell not long after, but even to this day I cannot walk past my old house without looking up at my old bedroom, half expecting to see something staring back from the window.

THE WISE OLD WOMAN

My parents had me late on in their marriage and I was an only child, but that never really bothered me because I had a Boxer dog called Benji, or Ben for short, who went with me everywhere.

One day, when I was about seven years old, I decided to take Ben for a walk around the graveyard of the Church of St Michael and All Angels in Bramcote. I had never been there before but knew that it was where my great-grandfather had been buried and where my parents had married many years before, so to me it was a place that I just had to see, and being that I was on my summer holidays from school, the timing was perfect.

I decided not to tell my mum where I was going and hinted to her that I was going to play with my friends so that she would not worry. So I packed my pocket with a cold potato for a snack and tied Ben to his lead as we set off on our adventure.

We only lived about a mile from the church but it felt a lot further to my little legs, and both Ben and I were panting in the morning sunshine, cursing that I had not packed any water for our journey. After what seemed like hours we arrived at the church and I can remember the sunlight shining through the trees and wondered how people could call graveyards 'spooky' when it seemed so peaceful.

Tired after the walk, I decided to sit down and eat my cold spud straight away, but as soon as I had settled down and bit into it Ben ran off barking, with his heckles all standing on end. I gave chase, alarmed as I had never seen him behave like that before.

The stupid dog was having none of it though, and before long I could not see him at all. Defeated, I fell to my knees crying. Now I was going to be in big trouble from my Dad for playing so far away from home and losing the dog! I was not really looking forward to the rest of the day and feared that my bottom would be sore from a thrashing when I got home. I had no choice but to keep searching for Ben, but I could not even hear him barking anymore.

I walked round and round the churchyard, trying to see if there were any holes in the fence that he might have climbed through, but I could not see any. I was just about to give up and go home to face my thrashing, when a lady all in white approached me. She looked very pale and I can remember thinking that her clothes were strange as it looked like she was outside in her nightdress. For some reason I did not feel right speaking to her and simply stood there with my mouth open, staring at her smiling face. I remember that she was not scary, and in some ways she had a beautiful peacefulness about her.

The lady seemed to be moving closer to me across the graveyard, calling out my name as she did so. At the time, the fact that she knew my name did not bother me, yet thinking about it now sends shivers down my spine. She then continued to tell me that Ben had run home and was safe and that I was to return as my parents were worried why my dog had returned without me. She also told me that my mother was to have another baby and that I must help her with the child. The old woman then pointed at my shoelace which had come undone, so I bent down and fumbled with the lace. When I stood up to thank her, however, she had gone.

When I got home, my dog was there just as the lady had said and my parents where standing in the kitchen with smiles on their faces. I can remember thinking that it was strange that I had not had a grilling from them about my day's whereabouts, but it never came. My mum set the table and we had cakes and a cup of tea in a matching cup and saucer, which is something that I never had experienced before when it was not a special occasion like a birthday or something. Then my dad cleared his throat to speak.

'Albert, I have some news about your mother,' he said, in an almost military style voice.

'I know,' I replied, 'you are going to have a baby.' My parents look amazed.

'How on earth did you know that?' My mother asked as she threw her arms around me. I could see that they were both very happy and so decided to say that it was a lucky guess, rather than tell them about the old woman in the churchyard. Indeed, I forgot all about the old woman until the day arrived for the baby to be born, when I saw the old woman standing by the side of the street, where I was playing marbles.

'Albert, go home,' she said. 'Your sister has been born.' As soon as she had said these words, she vanished before my eyes. This time I was scared but really hoped that her words were true. I ran as fast as my legs could carry me through the front gate, back door and up the stairs. Just as I reached the top I saw my dad smiling but with tears in his eyes, beckoning me to come closer to him.

'Albert, would you like to come into the room and meet your new sister?' He asked, as I hurriedly ran in to see my mum holding a pink crying bundle.

To this day I have not got a clue who the old woman was, but I have never forgotten her. If she had not vanished before my eyes I would have said that she was probably a wise old psychic woman, but with the speed of her vanish on both the occasions that I saw her, I have no other explanation than to presume that she was a ghost.

JUST POPPING TO THE SHOPS

I would like to share my own experience with you. It happened on Tuesday 19 July 1994 on Nuthall Road, Aspley.

I was heading to the post office between 9.20 and 9.30 on the morning of the above to get some stamps and envelopes. On leaving, I turned left to head in the direction of the Co-op but then changed my mind and turned right, going to the bread shop next door.

I was in the shop alone apart from the woman serving me. While I was making my order, the buzzer on the door went behind me. I looked around and a young woman of about 26 years of age had entered. I looked at her fully but not for long, but I do remember every detail about her. She was wearing a pink T-shirt with short sleeves and dark grey leggings. She had a shoulder bag on her right shoulder and was holding two white plastic bags crunched up at waist level in both hands. Her hair was 'mousey' brown and cut into a shoulder-length bob. Her eyebrows were full and her complexion a bit sallow.

She entered the shop and stood next to my right shoulder but slightly behind me. She made no sound or movement but I could feel her watching.

As I searched in by bag for the correct change, all the time I could feel the woman behind me getting quite close, and it was starting to make me feel uncomfortable. I turned slightly to pass without bumping into her, but as I did so I saw that the woman in pink was gone.

I looked back at the woman who served me and asked her where the young woman had gone, but she just looked at me oddly and said that nobody else had been in the shop all the time I had been in there.

I argued that the woman had come into the shop and stood at the back of me, but she was adamant that nobody had come in. It frightened the woman behind the counter but I did not scared, I was simply puzzled as to who the young girl was.

WOLLATON PARK

On 31 December 2005 my wife and I decided that we would take our two dogs out for a stroll around Wollaton Park. The weather was cold but clear and Wollaton Hall looked very inviting with a dusting of frost over the grass. We could not think of a better way to wave goodbye to the old year, and as we walked around the grounds we chatted about what the New Year would bring.

As we walking down the tree-lined drive our dogs suddenly stopped in their tracks and started barking madly at what seemed to be thin air.

My wife tried to calm them but the dogs were having none of it, as their barking turned into snarls and the heckles on their necks started to stand on end. Fearing that the dogs would never settle I approached them, but as I made towards them they just turned on me and started to bark at me, not allowing me near.

The next minute seemed to be played in slow motion. My wife suddenly let out a scream, and I turned to see what had scared her so. There, before our eyes was the shadowy ghost of a woman on horseback riding sidesaddle. She seemed to be wandering across our path and then returned to her starting point. Time stood still as both my wife and I stood rooted to the spot with the dogs still barking madly at the apparition in front of us.

As we watched her, frozen where we stood, the woman on horseback slowly turned to look directly and my wife and I, and then, as quick as she came, she vanished into thin air. At that exact moment the birds started singing again and time seemed to return to normal.

I had never seen a ghost before, and although we have walked the same path many times, we have never seen the mysterious woman on horseback again.

DIGGING FOR CLUES

My dad told the following story to my sister and I when we were young, growing up in Mansfield, Nottinghamshire. Through the years he has repeated the story a few times but the details have never changed.

When my father was young, he and a friend were planning a camping trip in Sherwood Forest during a school holiday. They were anxious to get the trip started and found they could not sleep the night before they were to leave. His friend's family owned a house in Mansfield very close to a very old and well-known cemetery, whose graves dated back centuries.

The cemetery was very gloomy and was protected by a high, wrought-iron gate that was locked every evening. The farther back you went into this cemetery, the darker it got. It was a moonlit night that night, and as the two boys could not sleep they made a bet that my dad could go further back into the cemetery than his friend. The friend took the bet and the two of them snuck out and climbed over the gate.

Off they went, further and further into the cemetery. They stopped against one of the graves a little way in, when my dad heard what he thought was someone shoveling dirt in the back corner. Hushing his friend, dad looked around one corner of the headstone and his friend looked around the other side. The moon was bright, allowing my dad to see the silhouette of a tall, thin older man, wearing a grey long-sleeved coat, standing over a grave, digging a hole. Dad sat back against the headstone and asked his friend, 'Do you see what I see?' His friend nodded that he could.

They looked again and saw the old man standing over the grave, watching him push the shovel into the ground and remove dirt, throw the dirt to the side of the grave and continue to shovel it away. Dad moved around the grave to get a better look, making a tiny noise as he did so. The old man suddenly stopped what he was doing and looked in their direction. Both my dad and his friend took off running for the front gate, never looking back, their bet forgotten.

The next morning, before they left on the camping trip, they returned to the cemetery and walked back to the gravesite where they had spotted the old man digging, fully expecting to find the grave uncovered and a pile of fresh soil. To their disbelief they found the grave intact, and there was no sign that the area had been disturbed and no evidence that anyone was ever there. The ground was solid, with no indication that anyone had been there a long while, yet both of them had seen, only the night before, an old man shovelling dirt and getting deeper into the grave.

DRAMA QUEEN

When I was 13 my mother died, and that is when my paranormal experiences began. My father then married my stepmother Stella and they decided they wanted to have more kids and raise them in Stella's home county of Nottinghamshire. I was the oldest at the time.

We moved to an old Victorian house in Arnold, which was, to be honest, a little run down. You could always hear people's footsteps on the floorboards, and generally it was falling apart. My father swore he would fix it up, but he never did. The house was really big, having five bedrooms, three bathrooms and two sitting rooms and a huge garden, which was perfect for me and my two younger sisters to play in.

On the first night, my youngest sister Shannon went to sleep in the second largest room, which had its own bathroom and French doors leading to a small balcony overlooking the back garden. At around four in the morning on that first night the whole family was wakened by Shannon running out of her room, screaming. We found her crouched in a corner of the living room, wide-eyed and frightened. She tearfully said that she had seen black shadows standing over her bed. I did not believe her story because my sister loved getting attention and making up stories. She wanted to be an actress, so she was a born drama queen.

The next morning, my father tried to coax her back to her room. She began whining and I took the chance to get the room, which was in truth the one I had wanted from the start. After a few months, when I was sleeping in my room, I heard whispers and laughter, which I thought at the time was my sisters playing a joke on me. I told them to shut up and threw a pillow at the direction of the sounds. I fell asleep again and then woke up late for school.

After school, I confronted my sisters to tell them to stop going in my room and making noises. My sisters Shannon and Caitlyn both looked at me confused and told me I was crazy. I decided to forget about it, and later, when it was time to go to bed, I locked the doors. I woke up at five in the morning because of a soft, childlike laughter and, to my amazement, saw a girl that looked about five years old standing beside my bed. She had long blond hair and wore an old-fashioned pink dress with bows. She smiled at me and I froze, unable to breathe or scream. Then she disappeared before my eyes and I ran out of room and went to sleep on the living room sofa. I did not went to bother my dad and stepmother because my she was a few months pregnant at the time. My dad woke me up in the morning and asked why I was not sleeping in my bedroom. I lied and said I had had a nightmare.

I saw the little girl many times after that, but she did not frighten me any more.

My second youngest sister Caitlyn said she sees the same little girl that I saw because she sleeps in my room now, since I have left home. I believe her.

DROP DEAD FRED?

When I was 19 I had a job as the manager of a restaurant in Nottingham, just off Maid Marion Way. While the restaurant itself was fairly new, the building housing it was very old. I lived in the small flat above the restaurant, which although not very grand was my pride and joy.

The flat looked as if it had last been renovated in the 1960s. Aside from a few new appliances installed by the owner, the shag carpet and lime-green walls with mushrooms painted on them had a retro, funky feel that was very 1960s–70s. I loved the look as it was always a talking point with my friends, and it was fun buying bits and bobs up to add to the look from the local flea market.

Soon after I had moved in, however, strange things began to happen. Initially, it was just small things that I barely noticed. For example, my alarm would sporadically go off in the middle of the day, even though I never used an alarm. The doors of my TV cabinet would be open when I went upstairs during my break, even though I never had time to watch the TV during the day. Lighters would appear on my windowsill in the bathroom, even though I did not smoke or light incense, so I thought one of the other employees must be sneaking up there on their breaks and snooping around. I started locking the flat door, because I was not comfortable with someone else roaming around my space without my permission.

After a couple weeks, the previous owner stopped by. She was a sweet old lady who sold the business because it had become too much for her. It was a slow afternoon, so I poured her a cup of tea and we sat at a table and chatted for a while. As we were talking, I mentioned the strange thinks that were happening in the flat and she told me a story about a ghost she had while she owned the restaurant, a ghost she named Fred. She said that back in the 1800s, he had been a city policeman and had been shot and killed while on duty. The circumstances were unknown. She went on to describe different instances where customers had seen a reflection in the decorative mirrors on the wall, or when bulk orders of meat, soup, etc would go missing from the freezer and reappear weeks later. I shared with her my few 'encounters' (as I now considered them) and she was convinced it was Fred. I had never had a paranormal experience previous to this, although I had never ruled it out. I always thought it was possible, but also understood the power of the human mind.

From then on, I made sure to never set my alarm, never open my TV cabinet doors and always take the mysterious lighters out of the apartment completely. I wanted to 'test' Fred, to see if he existed. I want to mention that I never felt threatened by his presence. If anything, I felt safer and at peace. As a 19-year-old girl living in a town centre by myself, I welcomed another presence!

However, I would still come upstairs to find my alarm ringing, my TV cabinet doors open, or a lighter on the vanity. As time progressed, I saw it more as a joke between Fred and I than him trying to upset me.

My most pronounced experience with this ghost came during one restless night. Although I fell asleep early, I kept waking up to my lamp being turned on. I relentlessly turned it off, but it kept turning on. Finally, I just said, 'Fred, enough! I need to go to sleep!' It did not turn back on the rest of the night. Later that night, I woke up to go to the bathroom. As I was falling back asleep, I felt the bed sink, as if someone had sat down on the edge.

I rolled over, and saw a pleat in the quilt, like someone was actually sitting there. Again, I just said, 'Fred, let me sleep.' Instantly, the bed released.

Throughout the summer, I continued to experience various 'pranks' by Fred, none of which were threatening or violent in any way. I no longer work there, but since then I have not experienced anything paranormal. I often wonder about the restaurant, and if Fred plays pranks on the current employees like he did me.

PLAY IT AGAIN SAM!

For as long as I can remember the cellar of my grandma's home in Newark has given me and most of my family the creeps. But you know how cellars are. Cold, damp, musty and just generally eerie. My grandmother's cellar is decorated with carpet and furniture and such as it used to be storerooms when the building had been a shop many years before.

Now, after many years of living there, the cellar is used for storage and is filled with piles and piles of junk. The only thing that is really of use down there is the freezer and fridge, and also the piano, which there was not room for in the house. I have played the piano since I was a small child and I very often go downstairs to play. However, for as long as I can remember I have always had a sense of being watched or that I am not alone down there, and it is as though the feeling comes from the area surrounding two lockable storage rooms. Nothing has ever happened there, no one has died in the building as far as we are aware, but still I have always had this strange feeling.

A few years ago I started noticing something very strange and downright spooky. Upstairs, right above where the piano is in the cellar, there is a bathroom. Several times I have been in there and heard the faintest piano music playing right below me. Being a skeptic, with no belief in ghosts, on one occasion I tried to investigate and see what was happening, but I found no one was downstairs or indeed had been downstairs. The TV in the living room was on and so I thought that it must have been that which I heard, and I believed this to be true for many years, using the theory that I was hearing the TV in the lounge and that it was just the way it echoed that made it sound like it was coming from the cellar.

One day I happened to be in the house alone. I had just walked in the door and all the lights and TV and things were turned off because my grandparents had not yet returned from their shopping trip. I desperately needed the loo so I ran to the bathroom, before I had had the chance to turn any lights or anything else on in the house. While I was in there I heard the music begin to play below me. Needless to say I was really scared, as I knew for a fact that the TV was not on and that no one else was there. I left the house as soon as possible and sat outside on the step until my grandparents came home, making an excuse that I had forgotten my key as I did not want them to think that I was mad or anything!

THE BUZZING GHOST

I worked at Nottingham City Hospital as a nurse mainly on night shifts. So many times there have been strange occurrences during the night that just cannot be explained.

When we work on our ward, we split it in half. On the night in question I worked on the 'far' side and my nursing partner had the 'near'. During our break hour, I was discussing a story about a Japanese horror movie I had seen the night before. It was about a nurse working on a night shift like us and how the call bell to a room that used to be occupied by a patient that passed away that day started to ring. She went anyway and ended up comforting a ghost that was in pain. She embraced the fact that her job was 'the Comforter' – regardless of the dead or living. I thought it was a lovely story, even though it was classed as a horror.

The thing was I never got to finish the story, nor explain my agreement in the nurse's actions and her accepting what her job really was, because we got so busy afterwards with patients calling for this and that. Suddenly, the bed exit alarm button from the far side room rang, suggesting that a patient had got out of bed, and since my partner was busy with other patients, I went to help her patient get back into bed.

It was dark on that side, and as I approached the room I noted that there was no name tag next to the door of the patient. Usually our ward clerk puts one there when he or she gets admitted, but sometimes our unit clerk forgets to put one there. I got a little mad but that stopped when I heard a woman distinctly moaning in pain in a fairly loud voice. All I could think about was that she must have got out of bed and fallen so I ran into the room, turning on the light as I went in. There was no one there. The bed alarm was ringing and ringing so I went to the wall to turn it off, only to discover that the alarm did not stop. By then, the other nurses started coming down the hall to help and a nurse got on the intercom to the room. After many attempts to stop the alarm, she suddenly told me to stop, pray for the soul and open the window for it to escape.

Like I say, we had encountered many strange things so this was not such a strange request. By then, two nurse assistants had come in to help, and they saw what I was doing and stood next to me and prayed.

After we prayed, I reached over to the wall and pushed the button to stop the alarm. The alarm stopped! All of us looked at each other with surprise and relief. The nurse that was assigned to that room told me later that a couple of days before I went to work, a lady in that same room had passed away after being there for a couple of weeks. She had cancer and was in terrible pain. All she would do all day and night was loudly moan in pain.

ANGEL OR DEMON?

My name is Sean and I am 16 years old, and I was born with a 'third eye'. I have always lived in Mansfield, Nottinghamshire. The 'third eye' runs weakly in my family, most just being occasionally aware of spiritual presences. I, on the other hand, was born with the innate ability to both sense them and physically see them – and even occasionally speak with them. I have been seeing ghosts my entire life. My mum even mentioned that as a baby and toddler I used to play with some unseen person. But my tale is about one particular ghost...a very special ghost.

The first time I saw this entity was when I was six years old, when in my peripheral vision I saw black hair and the hem of a white dress. From then on I saw her everywhere: in school, in the road, outside the car windows, everywhere.

The first time I ever caught glimpse of her face was late September 2007. My cousin and I were playing 'wrestling' and when I was slammed on the bed, I turned to get up and saw her standing beside the bed within my arm's reach, looking down at me. She looked Chinese and wore a white dress and had long black hair. She only appeared for a second before disappearing. I told my cousins and we decided to sleep downstairs that night.

After that incident I began seeing her more frequently, and often she would whisper in my ear just before I would nearly have an accident. I began to think that she was a guardian angel. I mean, the white could have fooled anyone.

It was not until January 2009 when I began to doubt. I was being bullied by my classmates, and when I was alone in my bedroom, hating my life and the world, I would speak out loud thinking that she would listen and hear me. She never actually materialised and sat down to talk to me, but my bullies one by one got injured. They said things such as someone pushed them down the stairs or pushed the knife off the counter or tripped them while they ran.

I knew it could have been my so-called 'angel' who was doing it, but of course I did not mention anything. The bullies were getting angrier with each injury and were taking it out on me, when my 'angel' would pay them back for what they did to me.

It was not until one of the bullies was in a car accident, because the wheel of their family car 'wouldn't turn', that I finally got scared. I begged her to stop and she did. I was sure that she was not an angel, so I began researching on the topic, and my theories include her being a 'Shikigami', spirit guardians from Japanese mythology that can be commanded by their masters, or worse a 'Succubus', which is a female demon.

I still see her but now she only whispers to me when I am in danger and does not interfere with anyone else in my life.

ONE MAN AND HIS DOG

One Sunday afternoon I decided to take my dog for a walk in the fields at the back of Dunelm Drive in Calverton. It was a lovely day and I was really enjoying the fresh air and the peace and quiet, when all of a sudden my dog started barking madly. I looked ahead to see what he was barking at and saw a man dressed in Victorian costume, with a long dark coat and a top hat, walking towards us with a dog.

My dog did not usually react to anyone, but on this occasion he started going absolutely crazy, so I bent down to calm him. I looked up at where the man and the dog had been, but to my amazement I saw that they were no longer there. I looked up and down the lane but they had vanished into thin air. There was nowhere for them to have gone as there were fields either side surrounded by high hedges.

Bemused at what I had seen, I hurried home to tell my husband and he admitted to me that he had seen the Victorian gentleman and his dog too when he had been out walking. We have no idea who the ghost of this man is but I would love to find out.

REST IN PEACE

My boyfriend, Nick, is a person of many talents. One of those talents happens to be attracting spirits. He and I had just got together when he decided it would be fun to take me 'ghost hunting', and since I have never had a supernatural experience, I decided to go. Since we were low on money and time because we were students at Nottingham University, we decided that local graveyards were our best bet. So, armed with a digital camera, we set out. That night we visited three graveyards. I will never forget the third.

The first graveyard Nick and I went to was situated off a well-lit main road, and we encountered nothing. Nick would not let me go too deep into the cemetery because he thought it was disrespectful to the spirits, although this also meant that we spent most of our time in the streetlight.

Before we went to the second graveyard we decided to pick up my closest friend, Beth. The next cemetery we went to was small and rather old, situated next to a beautiful church. Once again, nothing happened, although we did get photographs of some cool orbs.

As we drove, looking for our next destination, Beth suggested that we check out a large graveyard that her eldest brother had been to. It sounded like a good idea at the time, until we arrived there. The place was much larger than I expected, and there was a lot of ground to cover. I got an uneasy feeling from the off. We parked in an apartment complex down the road and hopped over the fence.

We started walking to the back of the graveyard, where Beth's brother had apparently seen a glowing figure, when Nick thought he saw something and went to go and photograph it, telling us to go on without him and that he would catch up with us. We decided to walk on without him and crept further into the cemetery.

The night was fairly light; the sky was clear, the moon was relatively bright and I could see all of Beth's features from a few feet away. As we walked deeper and deeper into the place my feeling of unease grew. I felt like I was being watched.

As we neared a group of statues, Beth put her arm in front of me so I could not move any further, but she said nothing. I turned to look at her face: she was looking in horror at something next to me. I slowly turned my head to where she was looking, and there stood the figure of a man who could not have been less than six feet tall.

Although it was so bright out that night, the figure had no features. He was facing the statues and he was only seven or eight feet away from us. Within seconds, he heard our heavy breathing and turned his whole body to us in one motion. He did not speak, which only served to make things scarier. Terrified, Beth and I started to tiptoe back a few steps, when to our horror it started moving closer. As the dark firgure started looming towards us, we turned around and fled as fast as we could. I risked a look behind me and saw that it was chasing us, but somehow its legs were not moving.

We ran for a while before we realised that the shadow was not behind us anymore. We hid in between four bushes for an hour before a concerned Nick found us, huddled together and scared out of our wits. We took Beth home and I went to stay at his house. We decided to sleep with the lights on that night.

Oddly, my encounter with the shadow man has made me love ghost hunting – the rush of seeing something that I could not explain was remarkable.

ORDERS PLEASE!

I have had many ghostly experiences in Nottingham, especially in the Trent Bridge Inn. On one occasion I stood at the bar and felt all the hairs on the back of my neck stand on end and I had the strange feeling that I was being watched. Yet when I looked there was no one there except a man sitting huddled in the corner.

'What do you want?' I asked, and he simply vanished before my eyes. Shaken by the experience, I asked the bar staff about what I had just witnessed and was told that many years ago that the chef had hanged himself and is believed to still haunt the premises.

WHO ARE YOU?

As a child I always had a very vivid imagination, and I often got in trouble with my parents for 'making up' such odd lies and stories as excuses.

One night, it was around 10pm, long after I should have been in bed since I was at such a young age, and I decided to crawl into bed so that I would not get caught by my parents. As I turned off the lights a sudden breeze ran through my room. I stopped and shivered – I knew it was a poltergeist of some kind. You see, ever since I was three I could see things and people that no one else seemed to see. It often frustrated me but sometimes it was nice to have a world of my own. Usually when a poltergeist was around I was not scared, but that particular night something ran different through me that I cannot explain. There was fear – and something much worse.

The air seemed to turn stale and the smell of decaying flesh was everywhere. I ran to the door but stopped, thinking that it would just seem that I was making up stories. As I walked back through my room the smell got stronger as I walked past my mini sofa. I looked down and saw black hair lying on the ground next to the sofa. I looked up and saw my doll sitting there, which only intensified my growing feeling of fear.

I turned every light on in the room and ran to my bed and tried to fall asleep. I finally must have, but I had an awful nightmare about a girl being tortured terribly by an odd man. He hit her and a startling crack stopped everything. He looked down at the girl lying on the floor. Her head was cracked and she was bleeding non-stop through her raven-black hair.

The man turned to her in the gentlest way and touched her cheek and started sobbing. Then, out of nowhere he pulled out an old steak knife and stabbed her, and stabbed her, and stabbed her, over and over again. Then the man started pulling her over to a spot, set her down and left her there. I thought he left her there for good but he came back, dragging the couch and laid it over her, walked over to an odd old-fashioned fireplace, lit it and just walked out of the house for good.

I awoke with a start. I knew that the house I had dreamed of was not my own house, and I came to the conclusion that my terrible nightmare was that poor girl asking for help. I pulled back my covers and ran over to the sofa feeling my heart beat faster as I lowered my head to look underneath. There she was. I reached out to touch the poor deceased body, but it disappeared.

It took me a while but I eventually started to forget about the odd things that happened that night, and after many months it the whole thing seemed like a dream at the back of my mind.

Then, a couple of years later, the memory of that night all came flooding back to me. It was the summer holidays, and I remember being so happy to have no school for at least six weeks. It was very, very late at night and I was getting ready for bed. Yawning, I flicked the switch on the TV in my room, but it did not turn off. I looked closer at the screen. There, staring back at me, was a girl who looked exactly like the girl that was under my sofa, treacle coloured hair and all. In a panic I hit the off-switch again and it did turn off. Freaked out, I turned around and the she was, standing there in my room in front of me. 'Who are you?' I asked. But she said nothing, and simply disappeared for the last time.

CHAPTER 2
ANIMALS

Some believe that the bond between pets and their owners never dies and that they are waiting patiently for their owners in the spirit world.

Others believe that the energy of the deceased animal can be transferred on to the belongings of their owner, and some witnesses claim that they have seen animals that are not connected to them. Could this be that the animal is trapped between the two worlds, searching for their owner or their home? You decide.

FEED ME

In 2007 my beloved dog Harriet passed away. I had had her for 15 years and I looked forward to our daily walks three times a day around Beeston. We followed the same route and on many occasions saw the same people who often stopped us to say 'Good morning'.

Harriet had become my only companion since my husband died, and so it was Harriet that became my confidante and best friend. To me she was so much more than a pet, and when I sat at the table to eat my meals, I would also fill her bowl and place it under the table so that we could eat together.

When she passed I was unable to eat and unable to throw out her things as her death had hit me hard. About three days after her passing a neighbour called in with a pie for my lunch, as they feared that I had not been eating. Not wanting to appear rude I sat down at the table and started to eat as my neighbour put the kettle on.

Just as I had the fork to my mouth we both heard a familiar rattling sound coming from under the table. It was the sound of Harriet with her nose in her metal bowl. Startled, we both looked under the table but the bowl was still and so I continued with my meal. As I did so we heard the sound again, and this time I was much quicker in taking a look underneath the table. The bowl had moved about a foot away from where it had previously been and was lying upturned.

There was no way that my short legs could have reached it so I knew that I had not kicked it or accidentally turned it over. My neighbour was still standing at the other side of the kitchen and so it could not have been her either. To be honest I was a bit upset that I did not see Harriet, but I do feel that she was trying to encourage me in her own special way to start to eat again after her death.

PAWS FOR THOUGHT

A little while ago I found a house for rent in Mansfield. It was slightly weather beaten, the garden was horribly overgrown and the interior needed a coat of paint and new carpeting. After the owner had given us the grand tour, and apologised profusely for the condition of the place from the previous tenants, I asked for a few moments inside alone. All was peaceful.

I walked outside and nodded to my husband that the house was clear. House hunting for the spirit sensitive is, to say the least, frustrating. As soon as he was assured there were no houseguests from the afterlife, he said 'We'll take it.'

It was my 40th birthday when we pulled into the driveway of our new home. My husband was due to start his new job in a week, so the move had been abrupt and the trip exhausting. Toting the teenager, the dog and the pet snakes, we had made it through traffic jams, blinding sun that burned and blistered my fair skin through the windshield, and a flat tire. But, at last, we were home.

Instead of sleeping like most normal people, we decided to get right to work. After all, we had been sitting down for so long and it would take a lot less time to unload the van than it had to pack and load it. It felt good to move around after being cramped up and driving so long, so good in fact that we were nearly done after only a couple of hours. I went about the rest of the morning unpacking the kitchen and arranging the furniture, while my husband set to mowing down the hip-high grass.

Once I was done with the kitchen, I gathered the empty boxes and broke them down flat. When I went out the back door to take the boxes to the bin, I had expected to find the yard difficult to navigate through the tall grass and weeds as I could hear my husband still wrestling with our droning push mower out front. I broke into a grin when I saw what he had done. He had mowed a path from the van all the way to the back door. Other than a dozen or so steps out to the path, my walkway was clear. I stepped from the back decking, with the flattened boxes on my head, and walked easily towards the bin.

I was halfway from the house when I heard it. The heavy, fast panting of a very large, happy, slobbering and playful dog, which had run up behind me and slowed to follow at my heels. As I stopped in my tracks, I turned thinking I was about to meet the neighbourhood four-legged welcoming committee. There was nothing there. My head pounded from sunburn and lack of sleep. I chalked it up to exhaustion, put the boxes down and went back to the house. Looking over the garden from the back deck, I tried to process what had just happened. Spirit of a dog, owner not living here, should be attached to a human. It did not make sense. It broke all the rules I thought I knew of detecting spirits with my abilities. Then the unthinkable happened.

As I looked out over the tall grass in the garden, the grass started to flatten in four distinct paw print footsteps right before my eyes. I watched it, I heard it – and I ran back in the house!

THE UNEXPLAINED

My husband and I are Ebay sellers. We go to a lot of auctions. We mainly buy buttons and small vintage items, and sometimes we have to buy a whole box of stuff just to get one valuable item in the box.

Late one Friday night after returning from an auction I was at my computer with my back facing the lot boxes we had won that evening. As I sat doing some item research I almost jumped out of my chair as I heard a whistle behind my back! I turned slowly in my chair and looked at the window. Even though it was late at night, it was light outside because the streetlight is right in front of our home, but I could see that there was no one in the window. Also I knew the whistle was behind me and came from within the house.

I turned and my eyes fell on the lot boxes. There was an old hat that looked like it belonged to an older man, and as I looked at that hat I felt my hair stand up on my arms, I knew somehow that there was a connection to that whistle and the hat. The whistle sounded

CHILLING TALES FROM NOTTINGHAMSHIRE

like a whistle one would make to call a dog. Nothing else happened that night, however, and I forgot about the incident quickly enough.

We have several nieces and nephews and two grandchildren, and I try and do little projects with them when I have the time. On one particular occasion we had a 'sewing sleepover' and they had all made beds for their pets. Our oldest niece was in the dining room sewing and asked us when we got the little dog? I did not know what she was talking about. She said a little dog had came to the end of the table and looked at her. But there was no little dog that we knew of, and so the thing was dismissed.

The old hat had found its way up to our guest bedroom and placed with the many other hats that I collect in a glass showcase cupboard. This particular room has no heat or air vent and when it became full blown summer we would keep the door closed to that room when not in use to help with the air conditioning.

One evening we retuned home from shopping and my husband asked me where our dog was and I showed him the dog was under the table asleep. He thought that was odd because in the stairwell you could hear a dog whining. We both stood there listening and you could here a dog whining like it wanted out. After a few seconds it would stop. We looked upstairs and there was no dog, and the bedroom door was still closed to the guest room. My husband went and laid across our bed for a nap and I went back downstairs.

My husband called me in a few minutes and said he had heard the dog again. As I stood just outside our bedroom talking to him about it, I heard it too and I knew where it was coming from, it was coming from the guest room. Somehow I mustered enough courage to walk over and open the door. I saw nothing but the whining stopped. My husband and I just looked at each other, and neither wanted to elaborate on it. Maybe if we just let it go, we thought, it would be like it never happened.

A couple of evenings later I was by myself in the house, as my husband was working late. I was sitting in the recliner in the living room and it was facing the stairwell. All of a sudden I heard a dog's toenails bounding down our wooden staircase and I saw a small, silky-haired dog hit the landing and head for the kitchen. I felt like I was in a trance and I followed it to the kitchen as if to let it outside but it was gone. I stood in the kitchen in disbelief – not afraid, just mystified as to what was going on.

One morning my husband had left for work early and left me to sleep in. I awoke to the pain of a dog or something on my feet scratching and digging at them. I sat up in bed and the feeling stopped. I lay back down for a few minutes and it felt like something bumping my bed like a dog would do when it wants to go out. For some reason I felt like I should go and get the hat and put it outside, and so I did.

I went into the guest room and opened the cupboard and removed the old hat and promptly marched it down the steps and out the back kitchen door. I laid it on a chair that we have on the back porch. I stood there for a moment with the door open, not saying it out loud but saying it in my mind that the dog should go out too. As I stood there I could hear a dog whining, it almost sounded like a puppy. I could hear it whining but I could not tell from where other than it was outside now. I quickly closed the door and went back inside. Later my husband carried the hat to the bin. I felt bad about putting the hat in the bin, almost disrespectful, but I knew I could not give it to someone else and that I did not want it back.

I have thought long and hard about this experience and tried to come up with a reasonable explanation but I cannot. I know the items had come from a recent estate auction, which meant someone had passed on and their possessions were now up for sale. I have heard of dogs mourning themselves to death after their master died, my own mother's dog had almost done it. I am a Christian but I know there are many things we will never understand until we leave this life. I never felt threatened by this incident, more uncomfortable with it. I guess the only thing I can say about this 'haunting' is that it was a man and his dog who were inseparable. They were together in this life and the life after. It gives me hope that dogs that once were in my care I may get to be with again someday.

THE GHOST DOG

When I was six I got dropped off at my grandma's house after school in Mansfield. My grandma lived on a really high hill with a long driveway and trees on both sides. One day I was walking up her driveway when I heard a whimpering. I looked around for the cause of the noise but did not see anything.

As I continued up the driveway I heard barking and a huge dog jumped out in front of me. The dog was covered in streaks of dirt and blood but I could tell it had been white to begin with. It growled and barked at me but what I remember most were its dark, pitch-black eyes that stared at me like it was looking right through me. I was scared out of my wits!

All of a sudden the dog jumped on me and tackled me into the grass. The dog bit into my leg just enough to make it bleed and I closed my eyes. When I opened them again the dog was gone and my grandma and cousins where beside me.

A couple weeks later the bite had scabbed over, although no matter how many times I had told them, my family still did not believe the dog story. At about the same time I was talking to my neighbour, and I told him when the dog had attacked. My neighbour told me that 13 years ago on the day of the attack his white dog got hit by a car and that when he had died the dog was in a frightful state of dirt and blood. To this day I am positive that the dog that attacked me was the ghost of my neighbour's dog.

RUNNING FOR IT

I am currently living in Nottingham city centre, and although I do believe in the paranormal I have never in my 26 years experienced anything of that nature until recently.

I like to keep myself fit so I often go jogging whenever I can. One evening I was running my usual route, which is around the Castle pub. This particular evening, however, I decided to run down along the canal, and as I got closer to a footbridge I started to hear a low growling noise which sounded just like a dog. I could not quite tell where it was coming from, just that it was up ahead somewhere. I stopped running and stood there trying to look for the source of the sound, but it had stopped. I started jogging again in the same direction and the growling returned. I stopped again. I still could not see anything up ahead but the daylight was fading fast and so I decided just to turn back.

Two days later I was out jogging again. This time I had on my headphones, it was late evening but still not too dark. I headed up the same route, singing along to whatever track was playing, and as I passed near the footbridge again I had this strange feeling I had just entered somewhere I did not belong. That is the only way I can explain the feeling. I kept going another 50 metres or so then turned around and started heading back – all the while having this very uncomfortable feeling.

As I passed back near the bridge again I saw a sudden movement out of the corner of my eye. I turned my head and saw a big black dog running at me. It was only a few metres away at this point. It gave me such a fright I just closed my eyes and just braced myself for impact – but then nothing happened. I opened my eyes and spun around, ripped out my earphones, adrenaline pumping, but the dog was not there. At this point I just took off at full place until I got back home.

CHAPTER 3
POSSESSED DOLLS

Throughout history people have claimed that the spirit of a dead child has entered the vessel of a doll, so that they can communicate with the physical world.

Some witnesses state that the doll has a 'wicked' spirit within and that it wants to harm people. Could this simply be that the spirit is frustrated that they no longer have a physical body and they are not being taking seriously? Or maybe it is because the spirit does not want to consider itself dead?

CLOWNING AROUND

When I was 12, my family and I stayed with my grandparents in Bingham, while my father was away in the Middle East with work. Having spent my entire life in the south of England, living in the Midlands was very strange for me, but I knew it would only be temporary: as soon as Dad finished out there, we would be moving again. We had been there several months when my mother's little brother and his wife popped in to visit. Auntie D loved dolls so Uncle M bought her a little clown doll as a surprise while they were visiting.

One day I came home from school to see this little doll sitting on the sofa; Auntie had placed it there before they went out for the day. He was 6in tall, positioned to be sitting with his hands out, holding a 'jack-in-the-box' that did not open. He had porcelain hands, feet and face, those horribly realistic blue glass eyes and had a music box in his belly that played some romantic song like *When You Wish Upon a Star* or *Dream a Little Dream*.

The first thing I noticed was that this doll was sitting with his face toward the front door, even though the sofa was not straight on to the doorway; he was almost sideways on the sofa. Expectant is the best word to describe the look on its face. It was as though the doll's painted face seemed to be waiting for us to get home – or Auntie to get home, anyway. I looked at my sister, and we both shrugged, trying to blow it off. I did not know what to think, so I turned him around, buried face-first in a huge pile of sofa pillows. I knew I did not want it looking at me, even if I could not articulate that thought at the time.

We went to change out of our school clothes and when we came out the doll was turned back around, facing the hallway, where we could see it straight away when we came into the front room. Our grandmother was in her room changing, she had not come out yet, and our brother was out the back and had not entered the front room at all as far as we could remember. I looked at my sister, gulped and said, 'I don't care much for this thing'.

She agreed. I picked it up to push it back into the sofa cushions, and nearly dropped it – it was so cold! I thought it felt frozen, even the cloth body felt like it was solidly frozen. We placed it into a pile of cushions – and just as we did so the air in the front room suddenly felt like a walk-in freezer. I knew our uncle would be leaving soon, and that he would be taking that hideous doll with him, so I hoped the feeling of nausea would pass.

Yet that doll seemed to haunt us, my sister and I. No matter where we went in the house it was there: our room, the front room, the dining room, the cupboards in the kitchen. I even found it on top of the piano when it was time for my practice – I felt that the thing seemed to be grinning so knowingly at me. My first thought was that my brother, knowing I hated clowns, that they terrified me and had done since I was a very small child, was tormenting me; however, when I went to my mother, exasperated and upset, he swore he had not even seen it, let alone put it on my pillow.

Every time I had to touch it, to move it, that doll felt cold as ice, and very heavy...too heavy for such a small thing. Of course, my auntie loved it, and thought nothing of the fact that it was never where she put it. She thought with everyone around that either a person or pet was moving her beloved clown. Everyone else seemed to brush it off, as though it was the single most normal thing on earth: a doll that moved itself.

Everyone except my sister and I, that is. My sister and I got more and more uncomfortable around it, until finally I asked if someone could not put it up or something. 'I scares me,' I said, hoping that, even if I was a big girl of almost 13 I could rely on my well-known phobia of clowns. Auntie D relented and packed it in her luggage, I watched her do this myself. She zipped her suitcase closed and I breathed a sigh of relief thinking it would be all right now.

That night I woke up thirsty; it was about 2am and the whole house was sleeping. I got up and went through the hall and into the front room, heading to the kitchen. My grandmother had a very real fear of the dark and so always used night-lights (she would turn on the bathroom lights as well). She even kept the light over the sink on, in the kitchen, so the house was never very dark; of course, this made it hard for us to sleep, so often we would close our bedroom doors, otherwise it was bright enough to play in there and read. When I got to the doorway of the front room, I stopped. The front room was so cold I could see my breath. Sitting on the sofa was that damn clown doll. I took a moment to calm myself, thinking furiously, trying to be rational: 'Ok, I'm seeing things because the night-lights are on and the shadows are weird, or something...' my thoughts trailed off, and it took everything I had not to scream. The doll had rolled his eyes over to look right at me. His head followed. Looking back now, the doll had the same body language as a bored woman does when you ask her to 'please look at this'...it rolled its eyes in an exaggerated manner, peeking out of the corners at me, and then very slowly moved its head.

I was raised in a Baptist home, very faithfully Christian, so I made the what I thought was educated assumption that a devil had somehow possessed that doll. I prayed for strength and then told it in the most authoritative voice I could to 'Leave me alone, you're not welcome here. The Blood of Jesus covers this home, and therefore covers you, leave us now!' I walked over to the nearest lamp, trying to be braver than I felt, and switched it on. Light poured all over the sofa and doll, as well as myself.

The painted grin animated now, grinning bigger and bigger and finally showing me teeth. I am sure you all expect pointy, meat-rending teeth, but no, it had the most perfect smile I have ever seen on a doll, but that made it so much worse. I suppose I expected a demonic smile too, not this blandly beautiful, too-toothy-in-an-adorable-kind-of-way smile. Slowly, slowly he shook his head back and forth, as though telling me 'No'.

That doll and I stared at one another for what seemed like hours. That grin, gleaming in the lamp light, while I kept trying to blink it away. I rubbed my eyes, closed and opened them over and over, and still that doll sat there looking at me, grinning. I glanced over to the clock and noticed I had been awake about 10 minutes; I pinched my arm, hoping I was dreaming. 'I'm just having a nightmare,' I said to myself over and over, wishing it was true.

I was at a loss, and decided to go back to bed. It sounds silly now, but I thought if it was going to kill me that at least I would go to heaven. I hadn't done anything to this beastly thing, nor had I done anything to 'invite' in to the house such a diabolical creature. I then shrugged at it, went into the kitchen and carried my water back to my room.

The next morning I awakened to the glass on my bedside cabinet, and instantly thought 'It wasn't a dream'. Jumping out of bed, I dashed into the front room to see the light was still on and the clown doll was still sitting there.

His grin was painted on now, no more teeth, but his head was turned toward the bedroom, as though he had watched me walk by the night before.

I never told my grandmother or mother about it, as I thought they would not believe me. My sister and I are still uncomfortable talking about that doll, it gives us the goosebumps nearly 20 years later.

My uncle and auntie left later that week and took it with them; I never heard about any other trouble with that doll, with one exception. No matter where they lived, I heard that the doll always ended up sitting on the sofa. I do not know for certain, though, as I never saw it again.

SEE NO EVIL

My sister, my cousin Vanessa and I have always believed in the paranormal. My cousin once told my sister and I that there was a 'creepy' doll in her attic, in one of the removals boxes at the front of the stairs. Well, one day we decided to check out her story.

In the attic there were a bunch of old antique chests and a load of removals boxes. We opened the box in question to take the doll out. We carefully took it from its storage facility, but as we picked up the doll we all froze in terror as we looked at it. The doll had both of its eyes missing and blood was streaming from the sockets. We all looked at each other, confused and terrified all at the same time. It then let out an eerie, screeching, screaming sound. We threw the doll into the far reaches of the attic and screamed bloody murder as we fled.

The next morning, we regained our courage and decided to go back up into the attic. As we opened the door with brooms and a mop in our hand, there was that damn doll sitting on the second to last step staring straight back up at us, with its eyes back in and no evidence of any blood. We slammed the door again and ran into

Vanessa's room and stayed in there, crying for the next hour while holding each other tightly.

Ever since then, I have had a fear of all dolls.

SAVE US!

I was given an old doll from my great-granddad, who owned an antiques shop in Nottingham. He gave it to me because he knew I liked collecting dolls and he thought it was rather special. I put the doll with the rest of my collection up on a white wooden table.

Late one night I started to hear what sounded like quiet giggles coming from the area of the cupboard. I just thought it was my imagination so I just hid my head under my quilt and went back to sleep. Later that morning all my dolls were knocked to the floor, all except the doll I had been given from my great-granddad, which was sitting proud. At this I started getting really worried, and I was also getting a little bit scared of the doll and the room.

That night I decided to sleep with my mum because I was really scared that the same thing might happen again, and it did. I heard the same laugh, but louder. I walked into my room and saw the doll sitting, with again all the other dolls lying helplessly on the ground. For some reason I started saying things like, 'Please don't hurt me' and 'Please leave me alone' to the doll, begging it not to hurt me or scare me any more.

Then, to my amazement and horror, the doll moved its eyes. Its eyes literally moved. I was so scared that I grabbed my shoe and threw it straight at the doll and ran as fast as I could out of the room, screaming.

I found my mother and we rang someone out of the phone book, hoping to find someone who could see what was wrong with the doll and had experience with demons and such. A lady came round to inspect the doll, and immediately found something wrong, asking me to fetch a knife for her. When I gave it to her she cut the back of the doll and dug around and found a picture of a young girl. She said that the picture was possessed and the girl was haunting the doll. I looked closely at the girl's eyes then at the doll's – to my amazement, they were exactly the same.

After that experience I never collected dolls again.

A few years later we moved out of the house. When I moved the wooden table that the doll was on I found writing on the wall behind it saying, 'Save us, save us'. Could this have been a message for help from my other dolls?

LET'S PLAY

One Halloween when I was eight, my older cousin and I were playing in my aunt's room, who was out shopping at the time. We started to jump on the bed, just larking about, when we heard a strange noise coming from my aunt's collection of dolls, which had been given to her by her grandma. After cowering under the covers for a while we started blaming each other for making the noises, each of us brazenly trying to cover our own unease.

We started to play again on the bed and soon my cousin needed to go the toilet, so she ran out of the room and left me in there alone. As soon as she had left, I saw one of the dolls turn its head to look at me. I know it sounds crazy, and if I had not seen it myself I certainly would be questioning the sanity of the witness, but the doll, I am sure, started smiling at me. I froze to the spot in fear and screamed as loud as I could.

My older cousin came running into the room and asked what had happened.

I was crying and so she came over to me and put her arms around me. Then she had a feeling that the doll was staring at her, too. She jumped on the bed and turned on the TV, but we could still hear the doll laughing at us in a sinister way. It was strange, but even though we were scared we did not think about leaving the room.

When my aunt came home we told her but she thought that we were making it up as it was Halloween, but I would swear on the Bible that the doll was possessed and that it was not my imagination.

NIGHTMARE

During my lifetime I have had several personal encounters with the paranormal, or supernatural as some people prefer to say. I shared this experience with several members of my family when I was about 12, which revolved around a set of antique dolls. Although I was not the one who actually encountered the ghost I was there while it was going on.

My grandmother found a set of antique dolls at an antiques fair in Newark, and she bought them and brought them to her house. The bodies of the dolls were made of porcelain and their dresses and hats were a combination of silk and feathers; they looked very old. She put the dolls in her china cabinet at the top of her stairs. My older sister lived with our grandparents; her bedroom door was just next to the cabinet. Right away she started having nightmares. She also told us that she heard an old woman humming and a creaking noise like a rocking chair while she was trying to go to sleep. She prayed and tried to ignore it until she finally fell asleep, but when she did she had nightmares.

Naturally, the adults did not believe her. They said that she had only imagined it and that it was natural for a child to have nightmares sometimes. But she continued to hear the old woman and to have nightmares. We were all starting to get worried about her and, of course, my other sisters and I believed her.

I should say that none of us made any kind of connection between the dolls and what my sister was experiencing at the time. I remember seeing my grandmother bring the dolls in, but I never paid much attention or thought much about them. It was only later that a connection was discovered.

My grandmother attended a Methodist church. She had some people from the church get together during a service to pray for my older sister to try to stop her nightmares. After the prayer one of the ministers came up to my grandmother and asked her if she had brought anything different into the house. He said that he felt like there was a spirit that was causing the problems. Naturally, she thought of the antique dolls and decided to remove them from her house.

To this day I do not know what she did with the dolls, but I do know that as soon as they were gone my sister stopped hearing the old woman and having the nightmares.

CHAPTER 4
LOVED ONES

When a loved one passes over they are no more than a whisper away, and even death is no match for the power of love.

THE 'V' SIGN

I grew up in the same house in Mansfield that I was born in with my sister Helen and my parents Don and Ruth. We were not a religious family and my parents were very strict about not believing in things that had not been proved. Any discussions about ghosts and the like were strongly opposed and so I learnt from a very young age that there was no point in discussing them because I would not be believed. However, I had seen several ghosts in my childhood and had to deal with the fear of them on my own, except for my friend Adam who I could confide in.

Adam and I had been the best of friends since playgroup and we went everywhere together. In fact, I always said that he was the brother that I never had and would share all my secrets, including those about ghosts, with him as he could be trusted not to laugh.

In 1983 Adam was suffering from depression as he has just split up from his girlfriend and had taken it very hard. Everyone was trying to lift his spirits by telling him that he would meet someone else, but he would not listen and drove himself deeper into despair. Even I, as his best friend, could not get him to see sense and he started to talk about suicide. To be honest I did not take it seriously, which is something I regret to this day, because a few weeks later, Adam took his own life.

His death affected me severely and I soon sank into a pit of depression. I started snapping at everyone and eventually could not be bothered to leave my bedroom. I stayed in there for days and days, just lying on bed crying like a baby.

I was doing just that one day when all of a sudden I heard the door to my room open, and my first thought was that it was my mum coming in to check on me or try and persuade me to eat, but as I looked up, I noticed that it was not my mum at all but Adam, standing there with a golden glow around him. He was wearing the clothes that his parents had buried him in and he was smiling at me.

I know what you are probably thinking...but I was not asleep, my eyes were wide open and I was fully aware of my surroundings. Adam just stood there and did a 'V sign', which is something he always did, and said 'You've got to stop crying mate. I'm ok. I'm with my Grandad and he is sound too.' Then, with that, he vanished.

By now I was sitting bolt upright on my bed with my eyes transfixed to the open door, and from that moment I knew that the best way to remember Adam would be to live my life to the full – and that is exactly what I am doing.

If that was not strange enough, years later when my wife and I were expecting our first child, we went for a 20-week scan at Nottingham City Hospital. My wife was lying on the bed and the image of our baby revealed that we were expecting a boy. We both were looking at the scan image on the monitor with tears of joy in our eyes, when all of a sudden our unborn baby did a 'V sign' at us, and at the same time a shiver was sent down my spine.

Thankfully, the nurse was able to capture the image for us in a photograph, and whenever I looked at the photograph and now my baby son, I remember Adam and hope that my son and I will be as close as Adam and I once were and that he is looking after my son from heaven.

A LITTLE IRISH DITTY

My sister and I grew up in a large flat above a shop in Arnold. It was nothing grand and we were woken every night by the sound of drunken men walking past the front of it. We did not mind though because the flat had three bedrooms and because my sister and I shared one and my parents had another it meant that we were able to have a playroom.

We would spend all our time in that room and were extremely proud of it. Our days would be spent playing with our dolls and William, the old man who used to sing us songs in his funny accent.

When I was about eight and my sister seven we did not play in the room much anymore, partly due to the fact that we had been given a new Spectrum Sinclair computer for Christmas and so every spare minute of the day after school we would play on that.

It must have been a good few months since I had been in the playroom but I needed to go in there to collect a toy to take in to school the following day. No sooner had I entered the room than I noticed William still sitting on the floor. He glanced up at me and started to sing his little song. Recognising it straight away I joined in too and was still singing when I closed the playroom door behind me and went into the lounge where my parents and sister were.

'That's the song that William used to sing to us!' my sister exclaimed, which prompted loads of questions from my parents of 'William who?' So my sister told them about the man who used to sing to us when we played in the playroom. By the look on their faces they had not got any idea what we were talking about and so I walked them into the playroom, but all we found were shelves stacked with toys and William was nowhere to be seen.

My dad turned to me and asked me to describe William and so I did. At this point my dad clasped his hand to his mouth and said that it sounded like his Grandad William from Ireland, who had passed away several years before we were born. He then asked my mum where their wedding album was as Grandad William had attended and it was the last time my dad had seen him before he died.

My mum went and fetched it and turned to the group photographs at the back of the album, when all of a sudden my sister pointed out William – and he was wearing the same clothes as he always wore in the photograph. My dad later told me that he was buried in the suit he wore to their wedding as it was his 'best' one.

We never did see William again after that day, maybe he was cross with us for sharing his secret or maybe he had achieved what he had set out to do and to be remembered by my dad. I hope to think that it was the latter, but one thing for sure is that both my sister and I are grateful to have been given an opportunity to meet a relative that had passed.

A BAD DREAM OR SOMETHING ELSE?

I have never been close to my mother's side of the family, except for her brothers and sister. This story is about my favourite uncle.

My uncle and I were very close for as long as I could remember. It was creepy sometimes because I was just a child and we would sometimes finish each other's sentences and somehow know what the other were thinking.

When I was 11 years old, I had a horrible dream that he died. I am not going to get into detail because it was horrible. But all I can say is that my dream scared the hell out of me. Three days later, my mum gave me the awful news that he had passed away. I started asking questions about how he died and how they found him. I was in complete shock and had chills when she described it. It was the exact same way I saw him in my dream! I cried because he was my favourite uncle and I loved him so much, but I did not mention my dream because I was too scared by it.

We went through the whole process of going to his wake and his burial, three days later. And during that whole process, I felt a strong presence next to me and watching me. But the night his burial took place the scariest thing happened.

I was laying down straight on my bed, half asleep. I was so exhausted from crying a lot, so I was a bit disoriented. I started feeling something on my feet. I paid no attention to it at first until something grabbed me by my ankles. I lifted my head up so fast that I started feeling a little dizzy, but I looked and I saw a man's arms and shoulders with smudged dirt all over. He was holding onto my ankles tight and pulling himself up on the bed. I was too scared to even scream. I covered my mouth and started crying but I could not keep my eyes off him.

At first I could not see his face because his head was down, but as he started coming up more I realised I was looking at my dead uncle. I remember seeing his Nottingham Forest football shirt, which he had been buried in only earlier that day. He finally looked up at me and all I saw before I closed my eyes tight was his long hair out of place, his eyes rolled back and dirt on his face. After I closed my eyes, the last thing I remember was whispering to please go away. I don't know if it was real or if I was dreaming the whole time.

But, the next morning, when I got up, my ankles were red and very sore. And there was a patch of mud on my carpet and smudges on my bed where I am sure my uncle had been.

GREAT MAMA

My mum grew up in St Anns, Nottingham, and was pregnant with me at the young age of 16. My mum was very close to her 'Mama', her father's mother. From the stories I have been told she was a very sweet lady and could not wait for me to be born.

Sadly, she died just three days before I was born, and since it was so close to the time for my mum to give birth, the doctors decided that it would be best for my mother not to go to the funeral because of the risk of putting stress on me, which could cause complications with my birth. My mum agreed, but she did get to say her goodbyes when the doctors said she could see the body of her grandmother, as long as she did not stay for long. When it was time for her to leave, she placed into the coffin a gold necklace with a cross on it, which her mama had given her when she was little, and left.

My great-grandmother had left her house to my mama, and that was the house that I came home to when I was born and that is the house I still live in to this day. My family was so hurt over her death that they decided not to tell me about her or speak her name around me. Well, she must not have liked that because when I was about two years old, my mum said I woke up in the middle of the night screaming like she had never heard me scream before, but by the time she got up and into my room I had stopped and was fast asleep again.

The next morning I was running around the house screaming my great-mama's name in a sing-song way. When my mum asked me where I had heard it, I led her into my room and under my pillow and pulled out the gold necklace with the cross. My mum screamed as it was the same gold cross that she had placed in the coffin, and she was sure nobody had taken it out of there.

My grandfather decided that I should wear the necklace, which I did for a while until it broke, but I still have it safe in a box in my loft.

I still live in that house, and I cannot ever imagine leaving it. I feel so safe there. I know she is still there, because of a little thing she does mostly around Christmas time. She will make the lights on the tree go on and off and I sometimes hear singing in my bedroom, like she is singing me a lullaby.

My best friend that lives with me has seen her a few times. I warned her not to play the piano that once belonged to my great-mama, but she did not listen and saw her later that day. Mum is the only one who can play it. She lets people know if she does not like them, and she even helped me get rid of a boyfriend I once had by scaring him half to death. Even though we still remained friends he still will not set foot in my house!

Although I usually see her inside the house, I have also seen her outside the house on one occasion. In December 2009 I was in a car with my cousin and his girlfriend and we had a really bad crash in the middle of nowhere, on our way to Skegness. All three of us were knocked out. I saw my great-mama and she told me that I had to get out of the car and kissed me and told me she loved me. That woke me up and I managed to get my friends out before a small fire started in the car. If she had not been watching over me I do not know what would have happened. I feel her everywhere I go, every second of every day. She is not a ghost, she is my angel.

IN MEMORY OF RICHARD

When I was 19 I was just living the good life, everything was perfect. I went to Nottingham University and was having the time of my life.

After lectures one day and I stayed in the library looking for a book. Waiting for a taxi after I had checked it out, I noticed a man watching me from across the street. I guessed he was about 23 years old, he was tall muscular with black hair. He was staring at me uncomfortably, but then when I looked at him he smiled at me.

A taxi came and I got in it, and while I was being driven along I could not stop thinking about the young man I had seen. He was handsome, but for some reason every time I thought of him, it gave me eerie shivers all over my body.

When I got home it was 10pm. I went straight to my room and read the book I had taken from the library and fell asleep. I was dreaming, it was not a nightmare at all, but it was about the guy I had seen across the street earlier. He was smiling at me, his eyes were chocolate brown and his smile was beautiful. Then, all of a sudden, he pushed me and I fell to the floor. At that point I woke up sweating, breathing hard. 'What was that suppose to mean?' I thought to myself.

The next day I took another taxi to campus, reading my book along the way. I live 40 minutes away, so I always wake up early. I got to my lecture room, and just as I was about to open the door I saw the young man from my dream was right there standing outside the taxi. He reached out and opened the door for me. 'Thanks,' I said.

'Your welcome,' he said with a smile. 'I'm Richard by the way, and I work in the restaurant over there.' As he pointed I noticed he was a very attractive man with chocolate brown eyes, long eyelashes, full lips and he had a heart-shaped face.

'Were you that guy yesterday staring at me after Uni?' I asked him.

'Umm…Yes, sorry if it made you uncomfortable, I didn't mean to.' He replied.

'It's okay.'

After the lecture it was time to go home, so I hurried out of the campus expecting him to be there. I was right, there he was standing outside with flowers in his hand. I walked up to him and said 'Umm…for me? Why?'

He giggled, took my hand and gave me the flowers. 'Yes they're for you. I know it is awkward but I just wanted to let you know that your special to me.' He was right – I did feel uncomfortable. He could tell that I was feeling a little uneasy, so he called a taxi for me and opened the door.

'Richard?' I said, 'We've only known each other for a day and I want you to know that I just want to be friends with you for now.'

'I understand,' he said, in a low voice. I got in the taxi and went home.

I went home and chatted with my mum before going to bed as I was really tired. I started dreaming again about Richard and this time he was not smiling. He was sitting on a chair crying, so I went up to him and asked him what was the matter. He lifted his head up and to my horror I saw that his face was burned! He then got up and said 'I'll always be here.' I woke up screaming and started to cry. I turned on the lights and remained awake for the rest of the night.

I went to Uni the next day feeling depression all around me. Richard was not there. As I was walking into campus I noticed there was an ambulance across the street, and I wondered why it was there. Then, in a flash, I thought about my dream – had anything happened to Richard? I ran to the restaurant where he worked and asked the nearest person what had happened. He told me how the oven had blown up and someone had been badly burnt. I was praying it was not Richard, but it was no use. I did not even know him properly, but I felt like I had lost a loved one.

Now I am 27 years old and married with one daughter. Since I got married I have felt Richard's presence a couple times. But I do not regret anything and I know he is always looking after me. To be honest I see him more as my angel or my guardian.

NO SOUL

About four years ago my great-aunt's husband went into Nottingham City hospital. I was with my friends at the time, who lived next door to my great-aunt.

We were chatting in the garden, when we saw an ambulance pull up outside my relatives' house, and so naturally I went round to see if everything was ok. The paramedics were bringing my great-uncle out, and he looked...I cannot really find words for it, except to say, he looked like a man without a soul. I watched them wheel him into the ambulance, and I called my mother's mobile phone to tell her what was happening. She laughed and said they did that once a week as he had problems with his lungs from working all his life down the pits, and she said he would be fine, but I did not share her enthusiasm. I told her 'No, mum, you don't get it. Something is seriously wrong with Gerald. I mean, seriously wrong.' My friends could see it, too, but not as clearly as I could.

Mum kept telling me it was nothing to worry about, and I kept telling her that something was seriously wrong with Gerald, until she hung up on me. He died the next morning. Mum came to me and told me and asked me how I knew he was dying, and I said 'He was already dead when they took him. I mean...he was conscious, aware, maybe. Mum, I watched his soul leave his body in that front yard.'

LOOKS FAMILIAR

My daughter worked in a firm of solicitors in Nottingham, and one day they were moving to new premises and all the staff were asked if they wanted any of the fixtures in the old offices. She decided on a picture of a young girl, holding a small bunch of flowers. She was a beautiful looking child and had golden ringlets, and for some reason my daughter was drawn to her picture.

The picture went home with her, and one night my daughter's father-in-law was babysitting for my her son, who was two years old at the time.

Every time my grandson saw the picture he would point at it and say the name 'Elaine', even though it was a name that he had never heard spoken at nursery or in the home.

His other granddad questioned him and asked what the little girl was called, and again our grandson was adamant that she was called 'Elaine'. The strange thing is, we do have a distant relative called Elaine who did look like the little girl in the picture when she was younger, but there is no way that our grandson would have known about her and we have never mentioned her name because she is not a close relative.

VISIT FROM GRANDMA

I currently live in my grandmother's house who passed away in 1985. She died in her bedroom, and when I married I also occupied the same bedroom, as it was the largest room in the house.

One day in December 2009, I finished my work and came back home late, at about 2am, and was so tired I went straight to bed. I dreamed that my grandmother was sitting on the settee with my young son, Amro. She bought a new school bag for him and was very happy to talk. In my dream I was going on a journey but she begged me to leave Amro with her and I agreed.

When I awoke, I looked at my watch and saw that it was 4 o'clock. I could remember all of the dream very clearly. It was the first time that I had seen my grandmother in my dreams since she had passed a way in 1985. I did not give any real though to it, I just took my lunch and was ready to go out. While glancing at the wall calendar, however, I stopped for a while. It was 6 December. I spent some moments to think about that date as it rang a bell, and I suddenly remembered the dream and that my grandmother had died sometime in December 1985. I was not sure on the exact date, so I decided to visit my mum to ask her.

When I told my mum about the dream, she told me that my grandmother had died on 5 December not 6 December, but I asked her to search in my father's diary to confirm it. She was surprised, but agreed to open his cupboard to see. When she found the diary, she opened the page of comments so we could read together what my father wrote. It said that my grandmother died on 6 December 1985 at 4 o'clock in my present house and in the same room.

I was very surprised that my grandmother visited me on the same date that she has passed away and exactly the same time of her death.

I believe that this dream was not simply coincidence. I believe she came to visit me and that our relatives who have passed away like to visit us through dreams so not to frighten us.

MESSAGES FROM HEAVEN

The following occured on Sunday 14 October 1987, and I know that for a fact because it was exactly two years to the day since my father died. I was paying a visit to his favourite park in Collerton to say a silent prayer and to remember him.

My father was a good man, hard working and very family orientated. He had been a miner, and throughout his career he had worked at most of the pits in north Nottinghamshire, so we had got used to him arriving home, covered in soot and coal dust with his whites of his eyes shining through in stark contrast. He was also an avid Forest fan and went to as many home games as his wages would allow.

On this particular Sunday I was reminiscing about him as I walked through the park, when all of a sudden I stumbled to the ground. Thankfully, the only thing that I had hurt was my pride as some children witnessed my fall and started to giggle. As I straightened myself up, I glanced down to see what had caused my trip, and to my astonishment found a piece of coal just lying there on the grass. It seemed to have been placed there and my instincts told me to pick it up. I did so, and I then felt a warm rush sweep over my shoulders, which reminded me of the hugs that my father used to give me when he was alive.

Noticing that I had tears streaming down my face, I decided to head back to my car but as I approached it, I noticed that the wind had blown a piece of paper and it had lodged on my windscreen wiper blade. I walked to the front of the car, still clutching the lump of coal in my hand as I lifted the wiper blade to remove the paper. It was then that I spotted that on the paper were the match results for Nottingham Forest! To this day I am sure that my father was sending me a message from beyond the grave, reassuring me that he was safe and well in heaven.

RELEASE

It all started in the late 1970s when my family learned a secret that my dad had been hiding. I have changed the names, so not to upset anyone.

It was a little after midnight and my parents were in bed asleep, and I was asleep as well in my room. Suddenly I felt enormous pressure around my neck, and I slowly felt myself losing consciousness. This sensation lasted only a couple of seconds but it felt like an eternity. When the pressure was released I started to scream, and my mum and dad ran in asking what had happened. I expressed to them the only way I could explain it was that I was being choked. I was struggling at this point to catch my breath.

The look on my dad's face was unforgettable, his mouth dropped and he exited the bedroom. My mother quickly followed and asked him numerous times what was wrong. He sat on the edge of the bed and told her 'I think it's time that I share with you something from my past. Something that I never really got over.'

As a teenager he and his brother had a best friend named 'Bill', with whom they always went out and partied. One night they had been driving on the A52 towards Grantham, and were going really fast on the road. No one had their seat belt on and up ahead was a sharp turn that no one was prepared for. The vehicle rolled numerous times and 'Bill' was ejected from the vehicle and died instantly. My dad told us that he had never wept or allowed himself to grieve for losing his best friend.

Just prior to my incident my dad had woken up to find Bill standing at the foot of his bed. He motioned for my dad to come with him, my dad followed, down the stairs, through the living room and into the kitchen. Bill turned and looked at him, still wanting him to come with him. My dad then just stopped and stared, and after a few seconds Bill disappeared in front of the fridge.

The next day we called the minister from our church to come and bless our home. He also gave us some really good pointers in reference to what we can do when we encounter a spirit. He said, 'Ask it what it wants'. If it is a good spirit it will tell you without hesitation, and if it is an evil spirit it will just disappear.

Needless to say, after this encounter my dad broke down and cried and let go of what he had been holding on to for so many years. Bill never visited us again, but I still wonder why he chose to visit me as well as my father.

TIME TO FORGIVE

This is more of a family thing that no one has talked about since it happened. I was born and raised in south Nottinghamshire and come from a very large Irish family. I have 23 first cousins! My favourite uncle was Uncle Mike, who taught me to do everything: how to be a man, husband and, most of all, a provider. We were always taught since birth that family comes first and to do whatever you have to do to provide for them at any cost.

So, of course, my family were hustlers. We ran anything and everything and if someone had a problem we had my grandpa and uncles to back us up, so needless to say no one complained twice.

Once I was taking care of family business when my dad called and said that my Uncle Mike was on his death bed. He had been suffering from kidney failure and had been suffering from stress as he was due to appear in court the following day. I dropped everything and went to see him. When I got there he was half the man he was. He told me he refused to die in a hospital so we moved him to my house. I still had a lot to learn and I wanted to spend every minute he had left with him.

On the way there he kept murmuring things like 'Those bastards have finally won!' and 'They're coming to get me!' Crazy stuff like that. The first night at home I stayed up with him, feeding him and cooling his skin. At 3am, he started screaming, saying 'Get away I ain't dead yet!' I calmed him down and he just lay there shaking like a leaf. I asked him what the hell he was seeing and my uncle just looked at me and said 'Unfinished business, son.' I had no idea what he was talking about.

The second night was worse. I sat there in the room with him and I started hearing footsteps, though I knew no one was there. I had told my wife to stay at my mum's and so I got up, grabbed the bedside lamp and stormed through the house, but I could find no one. I put it down to lack of sleep and went back downstairs. When I walked in the room Uncle Mike was sitting up in bed looking straight at me and said 'They're coming for my soul son, all those I hurt, they're coming.' I had no idea what to say after that. I just told him it was the medication and to let it pass. He laid back down and fell asleep.

The next morning I called my wife and told her about what I heard and what he said, and she was shocked. She knew about my family past and suggested that her friend, who is a medium, should go to visit my uncle. I agreed, thinking that it might put his mind at rest.

When the medium got there, she felt something right away. I still thought it was just a load of rubbish, but as soon as she walked in Uncle Mike's room she was thrown back. I swear, seeing this almost made me wet myself. She was literally thrown back, like in the movies. My wife started crying and left. The medium stayed. Uncle Mike was crying and cursing and saying 'Ok, ok, I'll go'.

The medium started to perform some chants and I felt this feeling of calm come over the area, like slipping into a hot bath. She told me that my uncle had done horrible things to many men and that they knew his time was close, so they were trying to take his soul. I asked why now, as he never had any ghost problems in the past. She said it was because he was too strong and now since he was weak they were taking advantage. Uncle Mike just yelled, 'I told you son, I told you they want me!' I fell to the floor powerless, then I remembered what I was once told about Jesus being able to forgive sins even if you are on your deathbed, so I ran out of the room and phoned the local vicar.

The vicar came round and sat alone with my uncle. I was not allowed to be in the room, but when they had finished my uncle looked peaceful and said that the spirits had gone. He lived another week but I am glad that he was able to make peace with himself and God before he passed over to the other side.

CHAPTER 5
ELECTRONIC VOICE PHENOMENON

Electronic Voice Phenomenon is the capturing of disembodied voices via audio recording devices.

EVP ENCOUNTERS

As well as being able to sometimes see or hear spirits, and having encountered them plenty of times when I was younger, I used to go to cemeteries and museums often. Some of these stories are not my own, but happened to a friend of my mum's, who is also from Nottingham. They scared me so badly, that I feel like sharing them with you!

First off, I have always loved the overall vibes most cemeteries give off. I find it quite peaceful and, even as a little girl, I would go there with my mum and try to leave flowers on the older graves if possible. But sometimes the graveyards felt a bit malicious, or just certain areas.

It was not until I met my friend at college that I started going again. Her mum had taken part in paranormal investigations before and liked to go 'ghost hunting' as a hobby. I was quite skeptical about these so-called EVPs they would get, but I think that I was mostly shielding my fear and gullibility. So, one day they finally shared some with me. I must say, some of the voices were so scary that I started crying. I know some were pretty generic: a moan or a 'hello'. But one that stood out was taken in an old cemetery in Nottinghamshire. My friend's mum had been drawn to a very large grave which housed a woman and her two children, who had died two years apart. She and her friend sat with the recorder for a moment before going on, asking a question like, 'What happened to your children?' What they found upon their return back home was pretty scary.

Upon listening to the recording, they heard the question, and then a strange sounding voice saying 'I killed them', then her friend saying 'Oh, 88 years!' and then a very distorted male voice saying, 'fun is over'. When I listened to it, I cried; it really was quite disturbing.

Another time I started feeling ill while on a ghost hunt and so I decided to abandon the hunt, and when we got back to my friend's house and we listened back, we heard me say 'yes' and then a man say, 'Oh no, are you feeling alright?' or something of the sort. It also happened to my friend, with what sounded like the same man.

I cannot recall all of the stories, so perhaps I will just list a few of the results we got. One time, in a very large and historic cemetery, we found a burial site that was made for religious purposes. They were Mormon, or Christian, something like that, and the whole place gave off a very 'strict', hardline sort of vibe.

We listened back to the recordings we had made there and heard a man yell, 'Witch!' We came to the conclusion that this was aimed at us. Another time, a friend was at a cemetery by my old house, and when she listened to the recording she had made, all she could hear was screaming. I swear, I made her stop because it was so horrifying.

We also got some very weird distorted voices, one in particular being a female who seemingly said, 'Hungeyshlim'. It was odd, but quite scary to listen to. Another one was of two children playing, one saying, 'I'm gonna getcha!' and the other shouting, 'Noooo!'

We also got our fair share of voices saying 'go to hell' and laughter. There was one recorded while my mum was with her friend, when they went to an old cemetery out in the country on the border of Nottinghamshire and Derbyshire. While walking, out of nowhere my mum's friend made a cutesy sort of noise, the kind you make to a baby or animal, although there was no audible noise of that sort at the time. When playing back the tape, they heard her make the noise, and then a dog bark and whimper excitedly! It was very strange.

I sometimes wished I had asked them to do EVPs in my old house, but if we had got any responses, I do not think I would have been able to sleep there.

The most frightening part in EVP work is the fact that, even though you are safe at home at the end of the day, the fact that you were there with the unseen is still pretty shocking. They might have seen you, while you had no clue they were there except for the sudden drops in temperature. And, there is always a possibility that one followed you home, so we made sure to tell them that they did not belong with us at the end of every session.

NEVER AGAIN

About a year and a half ago, my then boyfriend and I were hanging out at his friend's flat in the centre of Nottingham. This friend of his, Kyle, is in a band that are known in the local area and have released albums, and because of this he had a spare room made into a home recording studio. The flat was huge, with three stories and three bedrooms, and we would regularly chill out in that studio room. It contained very expensive recording equipment and a recording program on a computer that showed a flat line when there was silence and spikes when there was noise.

Kyle told us about how one day he was recording a sample of his guitar playing and playing it back, when in between fiddling with the guitar he thought he saw a spike blip on the screen and heard something in the silence of the recording. Puzzled, he turned the volume up and played it back, and he could hear a voice, almost a whisper, saying his name.

Next time we went round, Kyle played this back for us, since he had saved it to a file on the computer. I am very skeptical; I do not like the inexplicable and yet I heard this voice. Admittedly, it sounded like his name was being said, I could not deny it. But I still did not believe it. He is a recording artist, after all, and I thought maybe he was just trying a party trick on us. So he asked if we wanted to try it. He explained he would record our question or whatever we had to say, then we would sit in silence for a couple of minutes, and then he would play it back, turning the volume up when the silence would start.

At first I said no, but my ex and my other friend Molly, Kyle's girlfriend at the time, tried it in front of me. I do not even remember what they asked, I just remember a hoarse voice on the playback whispering what sounded like 'Toniooo' over and over again, whenever it was asked who wanted to talk. That was creepy enough, as my ex and I knew that his uncle, called Antonio, had sadly died only that week. Intrigued, and still a little skeptical, I let my curiosity get the better of me to give it a try. And I got the strongest response.

When it was my turn, I asked 'This is Shannon, is there anyone there who wants to talk to me?' I sat in silence for a minute. Kyle played it back and when he did I got a sudden deep chill. Not like I was cold, but more like an overwhelming fear which took over me completely. On the recording were several voices, all talking at once. I thought maybe it was radio being picked up. So I tried again, and decided to specifically ask for my great-grandmother, who passed away in 2001. She only knew Spanish, so I asked in Spanish the best I could. I will never forget what played back. It was her voice, but she sounded younger, like maybe she was about 40 or so. She died at 93, and her voice was then weak, as it is with old age. She responded in Spanish, saying 'oye me, oye me! essstass...aquuui'. That is exactly how she sounded, dragging out the words. I was completely gripped with fear and excitement at the same time, and tried again. Kyle stopped the recording, started a new one, and again I tried, asking 'Nana, its me, Shannon, are you here? Are you here?' Stop, silence, playback. 'Sii, esstaassss aaauii. Oye me!' All this time, the voices were still in the background of these recordings, getting louder, and more were joining, seemingly trying to talk over one another or to one another.

I did not know what 'oye me' meant until the next day, when I asked my mum to translate. She told me it means 'listen to me' or 'hear me'!

Frightened and kind of happy to hear her voice, it was strange since naturally I never thought I would hear her voice again because she was gone. But that is all she said in the recording. I listened to it again, however, and as it played on another voice came in. A deeper voice, someone else came through, louder than all the others. It sounded evil to me, like a deep whisper from someone's throat, dragging out every word. It first said 'Tiss youur hhheeneemmy'. Right after that, it said 'keep clear of Haaannnie'. At first I did not know what it was saying, none of us could, but after listening to it twice, Molly realised it was saying 'This is your enemy' and 'Keep clear of Annie'. There was no more happiness from hearing my grandma. I was so terrified I could barely talk, even with three other people in the room. I asked again 'Who are you? Are you saying keep clear of Annie?' This time the playback voice responded with 'Yyeeesss....khheeeep clear off Hhannie...'

Whoever this voice was, it was refusing to tell me its name or who or what it was. But what it was saying about Annie I will never forget. Annie was related to my ex. We hated each other, and she always took every opportunity to make me look bad or say something bad about me in front of him. At the time this happened, we were fighting with each other and not on speaking terms. No one in that room knew this. There was no way that Kyle could have pre-recorded any of this, especially my great-grandmother's voice. I was so scared of what I may have invited into that room, I was shaking. Asking around, no one else felt any fear at all. They felt completely fine and normal; it was only me. Hearing that, I ended the session right there, announcing to the entity 'You don't have to go home, but you can't stay here or with us', making a joke of it so no one would know how scared I was.

This is where my 'paranormal' experience ends. Later I was almost convinced that although the strange voice chilled me to the bone, it was most likely there to help since it told me things as if they were a warning against others in my life. The few that believed me were convinced too, and that I maybe should go back another night and bring it up again, but something did not fit. Why did it refuse to tell me who it was? It seemed to be warning me, but why did I get the feeling it was telling me what I thought I wanted to hear?

I have a friend, who is 'psychic', and told her about what happened. She was a little upset that I had done such a stupid thing, but agreed to look into it for me. Without knowing what happened, she called me back two days later and told me that yes, someone in my family came through, but only briefly. And something else did too, and it was, in her words, 'very bad'. She told me she did not know who or what it was, but that it wanted me to trust it, so I can go back and call upon it again so it can attach itself to me, or something strange like that. She said she took care of it, and nothing should be bothering me. But if I do decide to go back, there may not be much more she can do.

This is the first time, and hopefully last time, that I ever made contact; asked a question and something responded. I hear that voice in my head almost every day, and I play those chilling events back in my mind all the time.

CHAPTER 6
OUIJA

During the 19th century the interest in spiritualism was growing rapidly and it seemed that anything which had a spiritual or occult nature would make a sound investment, and this ultimately led to the creation of the Ouija board, a commercialised form of 'talking board' which had often been used by spiritualists and psychic mediums.

So enter two business partners named Elijah Bond and Charles Kennard who developed their own version of a spirit board, combining the French and German words for 'yes'. With their head for business and interest in spiritualism it was not long before the Ouija board was born.

A Ouija board contains letters, numbers and common words such as 'yes', 'no' and 'goodbye'. Users hold a device known as a planchette and supposedly allow the spirit to move it around the board.

Although Bond and Kennard are historically credited with inventing the modern Ouija board, it was an employee named William Fuld who took over the commercial production of the official board. Fuld, however, could not completely prevent competitors from marketing similar spirit boards due to financial restraints, although the name Ouija was a recognised trademark. When he died Fuld left an interesting estate, and in 1966 the manufacturing and trademark rights to the game were sold to the Parker Brothers. Today only Parker Brothers can call their product a true Ouija board.

The Ouija board itself is only a medium between the spirit world and the players, although some Ouija board enthusiasts claim the board itself cannot be destroyed. After contacting a willing spirit, players make light contact with the planchette and allow it to move across the Ouija board. Individual letters and numbers are often dictated to a non-participant for later deciphering. Simple yes-or-no questions can be answered directly.

Many critics of the Ouija board believe the planchette's movements are not caused by spiritual intervention, but by involuntary movements created by the players themselves. One or more participants may be forcing the answers, or the players' collective muscle tension could create movement, a phenomenon known as the ideomotor effect. A Ouija board player desperately seeking a spiritual connection with a loved one could also be subconsciously guiding the planchette towards an idealised answer.

There is also a strong religious objection to the Ouija board phenomenon. According to mainstream Christian thought, Satan could disguise malevolent spirits as the harmless spirit guides sought out by Ouija board users. These evil spirits could use the Ouija board as a means of possessing the users' thoughts or to cause personal harm. Prominent Ouija board critics have documented evidence of lives permanently altered following malevolent Ouija board sessions. One Ouija board rule warns against playing the game alone, while another suggests that the spirits must be approached in a specific way to avoid encountering evil imposters, and always a session should be ended with the appropriate closure and goodbyes.

I personally have never used a board, but I have been called out to many homes in which one has been used in order to spiritually 'clear up' and would urge anyone who is thinking of using one to proceed with extreme caution as this is certainly not a game.

COME TO PLAY

Seven years ago I was in a small drama club. The weekend before our performance we decided to stay the night at one of the girls' houses to practise our lines and hang out. Before I begin to recount the events of that horrible night, however, I must first tell you about the house.

Dee's mum (the names have been changed) had a fascination with ghosts. She had weird paintings on the wall and everything. She also had the little Hallmark Villages set up all around her living room, which were a little strange. Dee never said anything about her house being haunted or evil though, and it did not feel haunted when I first entered. I would soon find out how very wrong I was.

We started out practising our lines in her garage. We soon got bored, however, and started telling ghost stories. I really was not into the story telling because I had experienced the real deal many times at my best friend's house. While they were talking I was busy looking at the paintings on the wall. I found them a bit creepy. Soon I needed to go to the toilet, so I went upstairs, and when I returned Dee was standing on a chair in the hall trying to get something from a high shelf.

'My older sister was playing this game the other night with her friends. She said it was fun. It's not as cool as a wooden one, but it still works,' she said as she placed a folded board on the table. When she opened it I froze. I am a Christian and I knew what this 'game' was. In reality it was no game at all. It was a Ouija board. And I knew it was evil.

We followed my friend up the stairs to the living room, turned out the lights and set the board on the coffee table. I told them I refused to participate, but they did not really care as by this point they were so wound up with excitement. I watched for 10 minutes and then went to her room to watch a film instead. After about an hour they got bored with it and came to find me. I felt a strange, heavy feeling around me but I did not say anything.

Soon we all settled down in the living room. One of the girls, Penny, grabbed my arm and asked if we could talk in the other room. She told me she felt guilty about playing and wanted me to pray with her. I did and we went back to the living room. All the girls were asleep. That is when the grandfather clock in the room chimed. This would not be a big deal except that it was going off every five minutes. We started to get a little scared by it, so we went to the kitchen and played the board game 'Life' to keep our minds off it.

Soon Penny had to use the toilet and I went with her because she was scared to go by herself. When we were finished we washed our hands, and I turned off the tap and turned to leave. Then, just as we were about to turn out the light, we heard a metallic squeak behind us. We watched as slowly the tap turned and water came out. I jumped forwards, turned it off again and we ran back to the living room.

When we entered the living room, where all of our friends were sleeping, the little Hallmark Villages, which had been off all night, were on. The lights were all on in them and the mobile parts were moving. I freaked out and unplugged the plugs from the multiple socket. The room went quiet and dark. Five minutes later they turned back on. We were really scared now.

'What did you guys ask it?' I asked Penny.

'We asked it to come play,' she said tearfully. I could not believe it. I had not played and yet it was happening to me while the other girls slept. We tried to wake the girls up but none of them stirred. It was like they were drunk.

Things kept happening. The paintings of the ghostly figures rocked on the walls and the TV kept switching channels. We ended up hiding under the kitchen table with blankets and a torch. Everything settled down and we woke up still under the kitchen table.

We told the rest of the group what happened the next morning, but only a few of them believed us because they remembered us waking them and seeing the lights in a hazy state. Later we told Dee's mum, but she just told us we were making it all up. I just want to warn everyone that Ouija boards are dangerous and evil. If you see a friend playing with one – run!

THE WORST NIGHT OF MY LIFE

I am 30 years old now, but I have a true story to tell from when I was 17, almost 15 years ago, and went to stay in New Basford, Nottingham.

It was raining heavily all day, overcast and dark early, which is typical for a British September. I decided to call one of my friends, who lived in New Basford, who I had not seen in a while and wanted to catch up with. I gave him a quick call and he invited me to stay for a few days. I grabbed my sleeping bag and my toothbrush, and jumped into my rusted out old bomb of a car and headed two hours north.

When I got there, Jake, my friend, who was 18 at the time, had people over he knew, called Amber, Crissy and Mike. Jake lived in a big house he had inherited from his late grandfather, and his dad lived almost 200 miles away in Scotland, so we had the place to ourselves.

Although the house had a fireplace and wood stove, it was always cold, probably because of the high ceilings, stone and timber floors and open spaces. We hung out in an old wine cellar that Jake had converted into his guitar room and studio under the house, heated by a small blow heater, which was just enough to keep the basement bearable.

We were all laughing and having a good time, talking politics and music. The conversation eventually turned to more esoteric material, with Amber and Crissy talking about the occult. Mike and Jake were talking sports.

I was getting sympathetic glances from Jacob when he realised I had nothing to say about either topic. He turned his conversation toward me, and asked if I wanted to play a game. 'Sure,' I said. Amber broke mid-sentence and interrupted. 'We have a game,' she said, pulling a Ouija board out of her duffle bag. Apparently the girls had decided to stay the night too and had packed accordingly!

I think Mike was really tired because he sat out of the game, lounging on an old, beat-up sofa, and he fell asleep.

We turned off the one light bulb hanging from the basement ceiling after lighting a few candles and turned off the heater to create a more silent atmosphere. It was eerie down in that dark cellar, lit only by candles in the middle of the night, staring at a Ouija board in a big old house with only the sound of the rain and the creaking floorboards above us. But, surprisingly, I remember we were not cold.

We all put our hands on the board and closed our eyes. Amber, who was the one who studied witchcraft and that kind of thing, was directing us, telling us not to fall asleep but to relax our minds, to just let go and focus on creating a triangle in our minds where the spirits could come through. I thought to myself, relaxing my mind will not be a problem, but the rest of this sounds like rubbish.

I said nothing, but just did as she said. I tuned out everything except the sound of her voice, creating a space in the form of a triangle for the spirits to come through in. I felt sleepy, but I did not lose consciousness. Then it happened.

I saw an image of really good-looking man. I did not know him, I just remember thinking to myself, 'Wow! this will be easy to look at' as he stood in the triangle. I heard Jake make a quiet sound to himself too, like he was seeing him as well. Then, this guy reached out and touched my hand, I felt a cold chill run through me like a nervous tingle up my spine even though it was just in my imagination. Then the pointer moved! The image of the man stayed in my head even when I opened my eyes. I did not expect to be able to still 'see' him and keep my eyes open and watch the board at the same time, but I did. The pointer spelled out the word H-E-L-L-O.

Jacob was smiling ear to ear, as was Crissy. I wondered if they had a similar experience; I said nothing but I wanted to know if they were experiencing the same thing as I was. Amber just sat there, expressionless, and finally said in a flat tone, 'They have arrived.'

'Who? Who has arrived Amber? And did you move it?' I asked, but she swore that she did not. We all sat there silently looking at each other.

'OK, nobody move it this time, for real, let's ask it something,' Jacob said.

'Like what?' Crissy said.

'I don't know, something that only one of us knows.'

'Ohh I know,' Crissy said. 'That time that you and Mike went to the party and the car got stuck, Mike left and would not tell anyone where he went. Only he knows, let's ask it that.'

Amber directed the question: 'Where did Mike go on such-and-such day after he walked off?' Much to my surprise, the board did not hesitate, not even for a second. It spelled out F-o-o-t-b-a-l-l. 'Football? Mike ditched us to go to Football? Are you kidding me?' Jake was a little upset, I could see it in his face.

I tried to calm him by telling him that it did not matter and probably was not true anyway. The board continued to answer our questions for about half an hour before Mike woke up. He jumped off the old sofa and yelled something none of us could understand and scared us half to death in the process. 'What the hell's the matter?' Jake said to Mike.

'I just had a bizarre nightmare, I was at a Forest game and we won, I was so happy then afterwards I was allowed to go back and meet all the players. It was great, we were in the locker room and everything, then...their skins began to fall away, and they turned into vampires and crap and began eating people with knives and forks and drinking blood from crystal glasses. They sat at a table and served you up as platters of food. There were about 10 of them and they were digging around inside your decapitated heads, saying that if I wanted to eat the body, I had to eat your brains first. You guys were the main course.'

'Knock it off Mike, you're not very funny. Besides, where did you go that day after the car got stuck? Answer me honestly, it's important,' Jake said.

'Oh yeah, well, your probably going be a bit annoyed, but I went to play football, sorry.'

The room went silent and the pointer began to spell again. Y-O-U-A-R-E-A-L-L-G-O-I-N-G-T-O-D-I-E. Just then two of the four candles we had lit just spontaneously fizzled out and the room was plunged into darkness. A cold chill came over me, and all of a sudden I could feel myself being watched from every corner of the room. I wanted to curl up in a ball, because I could feel something or someone beside my feet under the old card table that the board sat on. I could feel the presence of something or someone coming through the brick stone walls that lined the wine cellar.

The feeling of being stared at from behind and from the sides was so intense that I had to keep looking around to make sure that nobody was actually there. The board spelled out again and stronger and faster this time, 'W-E-A-R-E-G-O-I-N-G-T-O-K-I-L-L-Y-O-U-A-N-D-E-A-T-U.

The image of the good-looking man in the triangle then turned into an image of a demon. I could see his dark black pits of eyes that sunk into his skull and dull grey cracked bald head and fangs in my mind. He was licking his lips with a dried out crusted tongue, scraping it across the gaping black maw that was his mouth. I felt a wave of nausea and disgust come over me. I closed my eyes but the image stayed there, and even got stronger. Opening my eyes wide did not help, since it was in my imagination I could not get the image out of my head. I watched as he reached forward and scooped out a portion of my brains, showing me and saying to me in my mind, this is your imagination, I'm eating it, and soon, I will have your entire soul.

I felt so alone and scared. Other demons with fangs and claws began to emerge from the background in my mind. Back in the physical room, it was filled with a thick atmosphere that you could cut with a scalpel. Mike was the only one who did not seem to be affected by it, he was just fumbling around in the dark looking for his cigarettes. The rest of us just sat there motionless at the card table, looking around the room. I could tell they felt it too.

Then, something suddenly slapped me on the back. I whizzed around, thinking Mike was playing a joke on us, but he was sitting on the couch lighting a cigarette. 'Something just slapped me on the back,' I said, looking at Crissy, Amber and Jacob.

'I know,' said Jacob, 'something hit me earlier too, I just didn't say anything before.'

'Guys, this isn't funny, I'm starting to get really scared here,' said Crissy.

In a flat tone Jacob just said, 'Nobody's laughing, I don't think this is a joke.'

Looking around the room I saw black, misty shadowy things moving in a controlled and very deliberate way around the walls out of the corner of my eyes. Some of them were lightning quick, and others seemed to stroll and take their time, as if they knew they had all night.

Amber, who was leading the séance, suggested that we close the circle down, and that this had been enough for one night and that we should go upstairs and make a fire and try to get warm. It was only then that I realised just how cold the room had got.

Amber started out by telling us to grab the planchette and repeat in our minds, 'spirits depart'. But the pointer just kept being drawn to the word 'No' on the board. 'I demand that you leave this house. Depart, now!' she yelled. The pointer just spelled out the letters G-O-T-O-H-E-L-L-A-N-D-D-I-E-S-L-U-T-S.

We packed away the board then, but the mental image of the demonic face would not going away, it was only getting clearer. I felt as if the shadow creatures I was seeing darting around out of the corner of my eyes had followed us up the stairs and were coming up through the floor.

I really started to get scared when I went to the toilet upstairs, turned on the light and went over to the sink. I stared at myself in the mirror, and I stood there for almost 15 minutes just looking at myself. I do not know what came over me, I just stood there in utter silence fascinated at the sight of my own face. I remember poking it and feeling it, as if it was not mine at all. It was the weirdest feeling I have ever had. Just then, the bathroom filled with a really bright light and my eyes began to hurt, like when you stare into the sun for too long. I then felt a warm calm brush over me and I knew in my heart that the spirits had left us for good.

TATTOO OF LOVE

I have always been curious when it comes to the occult and paranormal things in general and have been to many psychics throughout my adult life. I even used to attend a spiritualist church in Long Eaton.

My father had left when I was a young child after having an affair with my mum's best friend, and so although I knew who he was, I did not have much contact with him as he had moved away. To be honest I do not think that my mum encouraged much contact as she was so hurt by the betrayal.

Even though I did not see my father I used to dream about him as a child, and when I was 18 I decided that I wanted to get back in contact with him again and try and have some sort of relationship with him. Yet when I asked my mother, she was unsure where he was living as it had been so long since she had contact with him, but she did promise to try and help me trace him as she could see that it was important to me.

All we knew was his full name and that my mum was pretty sure that years ago he had moved to Preston, but obviously we had no idea if he was still there, so I decided to investigate on the internet, searching sites and contacting anyone with the same surname to see if they were related.

After several days of doing this, I had an email from someone who said that he was a cousin of my dad and that he knew my mum and wanted to speak to her. He had given his number on the email and so I passed it to my mum and asked her to call him. My emotions were all over the place as she rang as I was convinced that I was a step closer to meeting my dad, but no sooner had she started her conversation, her face dropped and her hand went up to her mouth and I knew that something bad had happened.

When she came off the phone she told me that my dad had been killed in a motorbike accident two years before. Obviously, I was extremely upset at the realization that I had left it too late.

Several years after making this terrible discovery, I decided that I wanted to have a go with an Ouija board to see if I could contact my dead father, and so I borrowed one from a friend. My friend and I decided that we would try it on Halloween because to us we believed the spirits were closer to the living on that night. We sat on the floor and started asking questions, when the spirit of a man called Troy came through. He was really angry and kept on spelling out swear words on the board and then moved the glass so fast that it shot off the board and fell to the floor, smashing it into little pieces.

Both my friend and I were really scared and ran out of the room, but part of me was upset that my dad had not come through to speak to me and so we made a pact to go to a spiritualist church in Long Eaton the following week.

I was really looking forward to the service when I walked through the church door and decided to sit near the front, so that I could see the Medium better. The Medium started to talk and she looked directly at me and said that she had a message from my dad. Obviously, I immediately sat up and took notice as she continued to tell me he knew I had been looking for him and was sorry that he had not been there for me. He also said that he knew I had been on the Ouija board and that it was him who had smashed the glass to rid the room of 'the angry spirit.' He also told me that he would send me a sign and when I got it, I should try and find a photograph of him.

I left the service feeling better than I had done in ages and knew in my heart that the Medium had contacted my dad because the messages were so accurate. I went to bed that night and wondered what the sign would be from my father.

The next day when I woke up, my right arm was hurting just above the elbow and I lifted my nightdress sleeve to investigate. I was shocked to discover that I had a perfect outline of my name in fancy writing imprinted on my arm, surrounded by forget-me-not flowers. Stunned, I searched the bed to see if I had been lying on anything that could have given me the imprint but I could not find anything and so I ran downstairs to show Mum.

As soon as she saw it she screamed and said that it was the same as the tattoo that my dad had done when I was born. We both stood there fixed to the spot, and I although it faded within a few minutes, I am sure that it was the sign from my father.

WATCH

I am now 18, and my father recently told me the story of something that had happened when I was seven. This is what my father explained to me – why it was his fault he almost killed me.

My father was only a teenager, 14 years old, and I suppose he did not know any better. He was walking around with his cousin one day, who was about two years older then my father, and decided to take him to his friend's house. I call this good friend of my father's cousin 'Uncle'.

They were just hanging out and Uncle had decided to call his sister's friend to come over, who was 15 years old. When she came over she brought an Ouija board with her, and they decided they would play with it.

When the began playing and asking questions, one spirit named 'Doe' told them on the board that he was angry with them for disturbing him. When that happened my father told me he had let go of the pointer, out of fear, but Uncle, his cousin and the girl did not. They told the spirit they all believe in God and he would protect them. Doe then moved the triangle to W-A-T-C-H.

Many years later, my father was now 22 and was in the Air Force, and Uncle was mourning the loss of his unborn child. His wife had just had a miscarriage; the child was strangled with its umbilical cord while in the womb.

My dad's cousin's wife had also lost their firstborn in a car accident when she was pregnant. My Uncle's friend who had also been playing with the board had moved to America and her child was desperately ill. She then also tragically lost her child due to a hospital error. She was so distressed that she later committed suicide.

My father had heard the news and remembered what the spirit, Doe, had said. When my father was 35, he married my mother and when she was expecting me he became really worried. His fears were realised as I nearly died in my mother's womb due to an infection that she contracted when pregnant, which led to me being born prematurely.

My father later told me he was scared out of his mind that he would lose me like the others and became overprotective of me. I finally had a reason why they had kept me out of activities such as sports, and why I was not even aloud to play in the back garden without my father's watchful eyes.

After seven years passed, my father had started to forget and I was soon able to play on my own. I was in the front garden one day just poking the ground with a stick and jabbing the grass with friends from school. I was next to a very old brick wall that held a pillar. All I remember from that time was pretending a toy car was a fighter jet, then all of a sudden blacking out.

My father told me the rest of the story. He said a brick had slipped loose and had hit me with the pointed end right on my head, which cracked my head open. I had stitches and they had put coverings over the deep gash it had made. I was in the hospital for about a week, in and out of consciousness due to the drugs they had given me.

My father had told me that it was a horrible accident for 10 years of my life, but when I mentioned that I wanted to try an Ouija board, that was when he told me this story. I certainly gained a new respect for the dead and decided that they were not to played with after all.

OUIJA BOARD DEMONS

My name is Aaron. I am 24 years old and live near Newstead Abbey, in Nottinghamshire.

The first time I played with a Ouija board I was 16. I played alone in my room with the lights off. I had a back light on so I would not be as scared, but as it turned out later on that did not actually help me at all. I started playing with it and did not know much about it at the time, I just knew all it did was allow you to talk to spirits and stuff. I was told to play with it around 3am, mocking the time when Christ died. One of my friends said that is when you know what you are playing is not a game.

I started asking 'Is there anybody here?' Nothing happened at first, so I asked again 'Is there anybody here?' I waited a little bit and then with my fingers barely on the glass piece it started to move. It said 'Yes', then I asked 'How many spirits are with me?' It moved to the number six. I wanted to stop playing right there and then, but I just kept going for some reason. When I asked if I was talking to good spirits, all it did was go around and around on the board not wanting to answer me so I asked 'What do you want?' It spelled 'H-E-L-P-U-S'. The hair on my arms and neck were standing straight up at this point. Then I asked 'How can I help you?' It spelled 'G-E-T-U-S-O-U-T'.

I did not have to think too much where this was going. I asked 'Where are you?' I got nothing but it going around on the board, so I asked again 'What do you want?' It spelled 'Y-O-U'. I asked 'Why me?' It spelled 'W-E-A-R-E-B-U-R-N-I-N-G'. I stopped playing right there and said I had to go. It spelled 'NO'. I packed it up anyway and threw it in the bin thinking that was that – but I was wrong.

Later I told my mum what I did. She started crying and went to my room to pray. I never saw her so scared before in my life. Later the next night I woke up out of a dead sleep. Though it was summer time my room felt really cold, and as I became more awake I could smell something burning.

I got out of my bed and walked down the hallway; nothing was on fire. I walked back to check the thermostat, but it was set to normal, so there was no reason that my room should have been freezing cold. As I re-entered my room I noticed that my back light was on, and it had not been when I woke up. I then started to get the feeling someone was in my room. I walked slowly into my room and looked around, including under my bed, feeling like I was five or six all over again.

I then noticed my window had been opened. I went over and shut it, and then, as I turned around to get back in my bed, my bedroom door slammed shut, the back light turned off and I heard my name spoken in a whisper right next to my ear. I screamed and started crying like a baby. My dad, a big man raised Catholic and ex-army, came rushing into my room with my mother and asked what was wrong. I told them. He thought I was just having a bad dream because over the years he has lost his faith in God, but my mum knew. She also told me that she was seeing things around the house, so I knew I was not going crazy.

In the nights that followed I started seeing a black figure out of the corner of my eye, but when I would turn my head too see it, it would vanish in a split second. I told my mum that I was waking up to my name being called, and that the back light would turn on and I'd smell burning. She said I had invited demons into the house and she said to ask God to forgive me for what I had done and to protect me. My mother had some friends from her church come over to our house to pray, and from then on the house became quiet again.

NOT A GAME

I am a 19-year-old college student in Nottingham and I recently had my first experience with an Ouija board. I really regret it now. I was invited to a friend's dorm to just hang out, but little to my knowledge they were planning to play with an Ouija board. I have always objected to Ouija boards because I was raised in a devout Catholic home. Anyway, I arrived there and immediately wanted to leave after setting my eyes upon the board, though I did not say anything. I'll admit that my curiosity took control.

We sat around the Ouija board on the floor. There were four of us, I have changed their names to protect them, so we will call them Chris, Jonas, Nikki and myself. When I first set my hands on the planchette, I felt a shock which pulsed through my whole arm. I quickly took my hands off and stood up and proceeded to leave. Of course, my friends convinced me to come back to play. We turned the light off, leaving a lamp in the corner on. I begged my friends not to call on any ghosts or ask any questions that we might not like the answers to.

We tested it; asking personal questions that only each of us knew. I asked about my how my grandmother died, and it replied cancer. She had died of breast cancer. My heart skipped and I knew this was real. We all stared at each other with big eyes and shock. Then Chris very quickly asked it how many people were in the room. It pointed to five. My friends laughed and made comments about how it was wrong. But I knew it meant there was a spirit in the room with us. It got worse from there.

Nikki asked who the fifth person was. I felt angered because of the promise we had kept earlier. The pointer moved, spelling B-E-T-H. Then she asked how old she was. It pointed to 1 then 9. I screamed for her to stop. Chris and Jonas agreed. I could tell they were as scared as I was. Nikki proceeded to ask questions. She asked how she died. The pointer moved nd spelled D-A-N-I-E-L. I felt a heaviness in the air and it was getting a little difficult to breathe. Chris asked who 'Daniel' was. B-A-D came the reply. The pointer then went crazy and spelled out, H-E-I-S-H-E-R-E-N-O-W-H-E-L-P-M-E. The lights flickered on and off. Then, the light bulb in the lamp exploded. We were in darkness. I could not even scream I was that terrified.

When I looked to the window I saw a shadowy figured walk in front of it. Nikki, Chris and I were standing near the desk, opposite the wall of the window, and Jonas stood at the light switch, which was about 6ft to our left. When Jonas turned the lights on, I figured out that none of them could have walked in front of the window due to their positions. I also remember someone holding my hand very tightly on my right. I thought it could have been Nikki or Chris, but I realised there was no one standing on my right.

Jonas quickly picked up the board and put it back in the box and left without a word. None of us have talked since about our Ouija experience.

STAY AWAY!

I believe that everyone should stay away from Ouija boards! I played around with one when I was 22 years old, two years ago. I have never written my story and the people I told at the time did not believe me. So I have just kept it to myself, until now.

I was visiting some friends at Nottingham University and we started playing with the board. I had done so before, but without any results – this was the first time it had worked for me. We were drinking and talking to it all night long. It was telling us a lot of true things that no one would know. You could literally feel the energy under the shot glass we used as a pointer, and it was obvious that none of us was the one moving it.

It told us it was a child around 12 that was stuck in between worlds. He had committed suicide. As he told us more and more through the board, we figured that his life was a mixture of my friends' and mine. This realisation only drew us in more.

Later, once all the booze had gone, only one of my friends and I were left awake. I told it to come home with me and I would take care of it. I do not know why I said that to be honest. I guess I felt bad for the little boy spirit. As soon as I said that, however, I got a bad feeling and so did my friend. He explained he did not want to play anymore and that he had never had this feeling before. I convinced him to keep playing and asked it 'Do you believe in God?' I kept asking it that until the shot glass was moving so fast it went off the board, and it was obvious we were angering this entity.

We both went to bed and did not talk about it again. I went home and met up with my boyfriend at the train station. He came back to my house, where we had to drop off things before we went to his house. I left the room and when I returned he said he heard knocking outside of my bedroom window. I did not care at the time.

We went to his house and he started to act really weird. He did not want to touch me or talk to me or anyone. We went to bed after hanging out with his roommates, but in the middle of the night he woke up, freaking out. He would not come back into the bedroom and said he was having troubles breathing.

Eventually I noticed he was fine and was getting upset that he would not come back into the bedroom, so I went by myself. As I was in there I heard two men talking to each other in the kitchen. Then my boyfriend came into the bedroom and told me he saw a shadow of a man standing at the end of the bed, staring at me. He yelled out in a panic 'You have evil spirits all around you!' All of a sudden he was fine and had no idea why he said that.

Confused, he said we should go to bed. I lay down and within a couple minutes I found that I could not stop shaking. I was so cold, but I was sweating uncontrollably. I was irritated. All my muscles hurt. I started pulling on my hair because of the annoyance. I was pacing back and forth. I could not stop, and then I started struggling to breath. It felt like every five minutes a hand was coming inside of my lungs and taking out my breath bit by bit. My boyfriend noticed what happened to him was happening to me but 100 times worse.

I was panicking and started to see two entities in my head. They looked like monsters. My boyfriend told me to get into bed. He was holding me and was extremely worried. I yelled out that I wanted to talk to my spirit guides – and immediately I was fine. As soon as I had caught my breath my boyfriend and I started to compare experiences and noticed the similarities. We filled each other in on little extra things we were seeing like 'shadow people', voices and noises coming from throughout the house all throughout the time that I was suffering.

The silence and calm lasted about 10 minutes. Then, all of a sudden, it started again. But this time it was even worse. My whole body went numb and I had the sensation of pins and needles everywhere. I saw in my head a hand above me and then my whole body started shaking like someone had grabbed me and was shaking me. I screamed. My boyfriend grabbed onto me and started holding me. I was begging him to take me to the hospital because I thought I was going to die. I dread to think what may have happened if he had not been there that night.

I started gasping for breath and giving up. Partially because of fear, and partially because I had no control and knew these entities were so much stronger than me. I started telling my boyfriend my goodbyes and giving him messages to tell loved ones. I was calling on angels and spirit guides in my head, and the response I was getting was a voice in my head saying that I have no angels that spirit guides do not exist. My boyfriend grabbed me and hugged me and started coaching me to breath properly. He talked to me for an hour as I cried, motionless. He made me do visualisations of loving places and things, telling me how much he loved me and making me tell him things I loved.

I saw in my head two beings starting to fight off these entities and I started to breath normally again. Slowly, after what felt like days, I stopped shaking and feeling cold and sweating. Eventually it was over and I felt exhausted, but safe, and my boyfriend and I went to bed.

My boyfriend tried telling his best friend what had happened, but as he did the radio turned on by itself and the volume went up. It was clear that these entities were not gone, and they stuck around for a week.

It was terrifying to sleep because of nightmares. I would have dreams that felt like I was awake and fighting a being holding me down, but then I would awake to the sound of people walking up and down the stairs and weird noises throughout the house.

I also saw shadow people following me down the street. My boyfriend and I felt drained and tired all the time, but we could not sleep out of fear. We did not leave each other's side. We had to force ourselves to eat as we were never hungry. And I started to think evil thoughts that I would normally have never thought.

My boyfriend was distant and would not tell me a lot of what was happening to him, but he would awake at night from nightmares and was getting haunted too. One day the freezer door opened up by itself and hit me, and finally I had had enough. That was when I knew I had to do something more because it was getting stronger.

I went to a person I knew, who is a spiritual counselor who has the gift of seeing into different worlds. She did not want to touch me at first, even with me not telling her what happened. Later she gave me a sheet to read to get rid of this thing. To my surprise it was positive but assertive, telling them they had to leave but thanking them for the experience and letting them go with LOVE.

While she was writing this I saw, under her door, a shadow pacing back and forth waiting for me to get out of the room. This woman told me she was protected and that nothing could come in the room that is a negative spirit or demon. The more she wrote and gave me instructions, the more I started to hate her for no reason and started thinking horrible thoughts. I felt like I was going to freak out for a second and rip up the paper. But I fought off these thoughts, as I knew that were not mine. I forced myself to eat healthy foods because she told me the entities were draining me physically, emotionally and mentally for whatever they had planned. I rushed home and began doing the visualisations and reading the paper as she had told me. It took around three days for these things to go away fully.

There is light and dark out there. Love and hate. That board is nothing but hate and dark. They will get close to you, they will tell you what you want to know, as they want you to trust them. But what they are after is to hurt you. Anything that lives and thrives off fear is not good and has nothing but pain to offer in the end.

CHAPTER 7
SHADOW PEOPLE

It is thought that Shadow People are usually attracted to one person or location, although the reasons for this are unknown. They are often reported as dark silhouettes of a human-like shape, generally male, that prefer to watch someone unseen and flee the moment they are noticed. Their 'personalities' range wildly from shy to downright nasty, but in my belief Shadow People are not evil or demonic. They simply represent a different configuration pattern than the previously documented orbs, vortices and ectoplasmic swirls and vapor that are the shapes of spirit energy.

It has also been reported that they have a tendency to feed on a person's fear, which can lead their behaviour to be seen as erratic. So if you see one, the best thing to do is stay calm.

IN THE WARDROBE

My name is Tammy, and I am your average 18-year-old who does not have a care in the world. I live in St Anns and have lived in the same house all my life. My parents divorced when I was three, so my dad and brother raised me. My brother and I slept in the same bedroom because I was just five and scared to sleep by myself. One night I remember that I suddenly awoke, and the room was dark, as usual. I remember looking at the wardrobe door and seeing a small, shadowy figure standing there. I could make out the outline, it was about the size of a toddler and had a cone-shaped hat. I remember it was putting things into a bag and it looked up and stared at me. I got really scared and started crying, which woke up my brother. He saw it too and ran and woke my dad up. He inspected the room, turned on the lamp, walked out of the room and went to grab a small Bible. He told me that it would protect me and to go back to sleep. After that I did not see it again and I fell back asleep. But that was just my first encounter with something paranormal.

When I was about 12 my elder brother and I shared a room. He would get home late and knock on my window to open the door for him. One night, I remember it was about 3.15am or so, he knocked on the window as usual and so I got up and unlocked the door. I went back to my room and he made his bed on the floor. As I lay on my bed, however, I felt someone or something staring at me so I opened my eyes and saw what I thought was my brother, sitting up in the gloom. I called his name but he did not say anything. All of a sudden whatever it was started crawling like a spider on my dresser, it was some kind of strange, shadowy thing. I was scared out of my mind. I was frozen stiff and could not even speak. I wanted to yell for my brother or dad but I could not move. So I did the only thing I could, I started to pray and say how it did not scare me. That really did not work, however, so I finally got enough courage to jump off my bed and run to my step-sister's room.

I lay down beside her thinking I was safe, but I was not. She had a shelf on which she keeps porcelain dolls and a Raggedy Ann doll.

All of a sudden the Raggedy Ann doll's head started moving forward and backward. I ran out of her room into my parents and started screaming, 'The bad thing is gonna get me, help! The bad thing is gonna get me!' My step-mother calmed me down because my baby brother was sleeping in the crib, while my dad got up to see if my brother was trying to play a prank on me. But my brother was fast asleep. I was too afraid to go to sleep in my own room, so I got a sleeping bag and slept in my step-sister's room.

After the incidents of that night my sister bought me a cross to wear, which of course I did. To my relief, nothing has really happened since then.

THE SHADOW MAN

I was all of four years old when I saw him the first time. I was staying over at my grandparents' house, and in the middle of the night and I had got up to go to the bathroom. As I came down the staircase I held on to the railing with the front door before me. As I descended, I thought I saw someone outside through the small window on the front door.

I had to know if someone was really there. I hit the landing, ran, ducked and pushed myself up against the door. Slowly, I stretched upwards on tiptoe until I could see outside through the little diamond-shaped window. There he was, blacker than night, standing on the pavement in front of the house. I could tell he was a man, wearing a raincoat and hat but void of features and standing very still facing the doorway. He watched me watching him.

My heart pounded in my chest as I slinked down from the window. I thought about running up the staircase as fast as I could and waking Grandpa.

Before I did I decided that I had better make sure I was seeing what I thought I was. Again, slowly I stretched up to peek through the window. There he stood, in the misty rain under the streetlight. I made the decision to be brave and not wake Grandpa from his slumber. I moved down from the window and went back to my pillow and blanket on the couch, although I did not sleep the rest of the night. Trembling in fear, I pulled the covers over my head and tried to disappear.

At breakfast the next morning I told the tale of my fear-filled night and of the man in the raincoat. 'That's the boogeyman,' my Uncle Tom, who is only seven years my senior, said quite plainly through his mouthful of cereal.

'That's why we have to come home when the street lights come on – he will get you if you go out after dark.' I looked at him and blinked. Thinking it might be a good idea not to go outside for a while even if it were daylight, I spent the day indoors watching cartoons and colouring pictures.

The shadow man has returned several times over the course of my life since then. Each time has been more frightening than the last, until I learned just what it was he wanted...

OLD RED EYES IS BACK

When I was about 12 years old and my sister was about six we had moved as a family to Mansfield in Nottinghamshire, though I did not like the new house to begin with. It had a weird feeling about it, although I would not have been able to put into words why I felt like I did.

In the beginning there were a chain of small events that were unexplainable, but, coming from a rational family my mum always seemed to try and make sense of it, until the paranormal activity became so apparent that it could not be dismissed anymore by anyone, including her.

The first thing that happened was to my mum, who had been home alone at night and was making something in the kitchen when she heard a noise coming from the bathroom. Upon investigation she found that everything on the counter, the medicine cabinet and in the bathtub had been thrown into a pile in the middle of the floor. This disturbed her, and when we came in from playing, she asked us if we had anything to do with it, which of course we had not.

Then, a few days later, when my sister and I were ready to go to bed, my sister said she saw two red eyes inside the wardrobe in the corner of the room. I did not see them, but I believed her because of how scared she was. We shared a room, and we had bunk-beds. My mum comforted her until she fell asleep. I fell asleep short afterwards but I awoke later that night from a small continuous noise coming from the foot of my bed (I had the top bunk). When I looked at my feet, I could see a dark figure jumping up and down at the foot of my bed. Every time that it jumped up, it would leer at me with a pair of little red eyes. The eyes seemed to sink into its face until the red would just disappear. I could not see much detail to its facial features, but I did realise that it was wearing a hat that was, oddly, a little like Charlie Chaplin's.

I tried to scream but no noise came out of my mouth for what seemed like an eternity, then I heard myself make the most deafening wail that I have ever made in my life, which immediately woke up my sister who then joined me in screaming. Within a couple of seconds my mum came into the room to see what all the fuss was about. Yet before she was able to turn the light on, I saw the little man hurry and run to the corner of the room and disappear into the darkness just before my mum turned on the light. We were so scared that we slept in her bed for the rest of the night.

A few days later, my sister and I decided that we should try and sleep in our bedroom again, but on the first night that we did I woke up at about 3am. I still had the previous experience fresh on my mind, so I very carefully peaked my head over the railing of my top bunk and looked around the room. To my horror, there was the little shadow man! This time he was just being very still and quiet, and he was just standing at the foot of my sister's bed, watching her. He then noticed me and looked up at me. I yelled, and again, just one second before my mum got into the room, he ran to the corner of the room and disappeared into the shadow. Every time he would run to the corner, he would stop for half a second facing the wall and disappear.

What I always thought was weird was the fact that the corner of the wall seemed to be the only place he could escape from. I told my mum what happened, and how he returned, so after a few more nights of my sister and I seeing this little man, my mum started to get really curious. We had seen him on so many different nights, she began to grow suspicious that maybe we were not lying or imagining it. What she did next, she did not tell us about until years later when we were grown up. If she had told us at that time, it would have made us even more frightened because we would have known that it was not our imaginations.

She told us that she stayed up one night with all the lights off. She was sitting in a chair in her bedroom, looking down the hallway to the doorway to our bedroom. What she saw next startled her. She said that about half an hour after she had turned the lights out she saw a shadowy little man come into the hallway from the bathroom. He started to walk into our room when he must have sensed something. My mum said he stopped, and slowly turned around and looked at her with those sunken in little red eyes. She said he then turned back around and went into our room. She hurried up and ran into our room and turned on the light. But he had vanished.

This was the last time that any of us saw the little man, and although we lived in the house for a further year, all of us, including my mum, did not like being in the house alone.

Personally, I believe to this day that the little man had to have been some sort of demon, not a human spirit. One thing that I never liked about it was the fact that countless times I would look around in the middle of the night, and every time he would be still, just watching us, either from the foot of my sister's bed or standing in the corners watching us. I never liked that, because you never knew just how long he could have been watching you as you slept.

MAN IN BLACK SHADOW

I know it sounds strange, but three separate people have seen a man in a black suit either in my back garden or approaching the front door of my house in Arnold. Now, this does not sound very strange but please bare with me.

On these occasions, when the front door is opened there is no one there and no sign of anyone around. The man in the back garden would have had to scale a 6ft fence covered with climbing plants to get into the garden and another the same to get out again (there is no other way in or out) – all while apparently wearing a smart black suit and with not a hair out of place. He usually is seen in April, and although I have asked my neighbours if they know whom it could be, they are unable to help me identify him.

This year I am planning to install a CCTV camera outside my house to see if I can catch him on film. I hope so because I would love to know who he is and what he wants!

THE GIANT WITCH

As a 77-year-old man, I have lived an extraordinary life and have seen many things, but none of the things that ever happened to me was as terrifying or horrific as when I spent my first summer as a 14-year-old boy in Sherwood Forest on a camping trip. The memory of that time still terrorizes me to this day when I think of it. I want to share my story with all of you.

It was 1946, just one year after the end of World War Two. My father moved the family (my mother, younger sister and me) from Luton to Nottinghamshire. My father was offered and accepted a job felling trees, and after the war we all packed up everything we owned to start a new life in Robin Hood's own country. As I recall the move took us about a week. I was excited and nervous about the move we were making. Little did I know at that time just how nervous I should have been.

My father had bought an old three-bedroom house for us, situated off an old dirt road about half a mile away from our nearest neighbours. We were surrounded by the tall trees that are common to the area. I never initially put much thought into it, but I had begun to notice as the weeks passed strange figures looming around the house at night. They appeared to be in the form of shadow people, and I would watch them from my bedroom window after the lantern went out.

At first I was not very afraid of them, just more curious. I noticed that the shadowy figures did not move as the rest of the shadows did under the moonlight. They moved differently, seemingly with a purpose. They also always appeared regardless of whether it was windy or not. I cannot explain exactly how I knew they were different, but they definitely were. They resembled people and walked through the forest in steps around the house.

I would go outdoors looking for evidence of their trespass, but I never found any footprints. I would occasionally find stones that were stacked up into small piles around my window. At first I discounted them, thinking it was my sister, but when I confronted her she denied it. She has always been very honest and sincere and I believed her when she said she did not do it. Anyway, at nine years old, I know also that she would not have been able to move a few of the larger rocks into place. My father was always working and never really at home, and when he was, he liked to read his paper and listen to his radio programs. My mother would not indulge herself in such trivialities as going into the woods and making piles of rocks, as she was too busy keeping house. So, the mystery continued.

As we lived so far from the beaten track I would often walk down to the main road to collect our post, about half a mile away. On the way, however, I would get a terrible feeling that I was being followed and watched. The further away from the house I got, the more intense the feeling. Sometimes I would run as fast as I could down the dirt road to get the post and get back as fast as I could. It was about a 20 minute walk to the postbox and a 20 minute walk back. I had managed to cut my time down to 25 minutes there and back and became a good runner because of it!

Even though I could never actually see them during the day, I knew the shadow figures were following me when I wandered too far away. I always felt that I could be taken at any time. I would regularly take down the small piles of rocks, and within a few nights they would re-appear, often in different places. And as I said, there never was a sign of human activity. I did not know what to do about the strange rock formations and the shadow people I saw. Every time I asked my parents about it, I was told to stop being stupid.

One night, they came really close to my window, I remember because it was a hot summer night and the grasshoppers and crickets were unusually loud that evening. It was about 9 or 10 o'clock at night, the sun had set not long before, and my sister and I were tucked into bed. As I lay there I heard a terrible thump on the outside wall near my window. I jumped out of bed and ran over to the window, and that was when I saw it – a black shadowy figure with a head, arms and a torso but no legs that whipped its head around and looked up at me.

I was so terrified I froze. Then I ran to the cupboard in the kitchen and grabbed dad's rifle, loaded it as fast I could and got to the door. I was so scared to open it that my fingers were shaking. But I closed my eyes and managed to do it. I turned the latch and the wooden door creaked open to the night. I took a very cautious and nervous step out onto the porch and turned right, where my bedroom window was, to look for the shadow figure. To my horror, there it was, still outside my bedroom window. Quick as a flash, I raised the rifle and fired off a round into it. I quickly reloaded the bolt-action rifle and got off another two shots before the rest of the shells from my pyjama front pocket spilled out onto the floor. The thing did not react to the bullets being fired through it, instead it just menaced at me, floating there by my bedroom window.

It was not long before my dad came running out to see who was firing his gun. The thing had whipped away into the darkness so fast in less than a second that by the time my dad was there it was gone. He took the rifle from me, picked up a few shells, reloaded it and pushed me behind him. He stood between me and the dark woods, where this thing had come from, and asked if I had seen a fox. I bit my lip and lied. Yes, it was a fox. 'Did you get it?' He asked.

'I'm sorry, I don't think so', I said, feeling bad for telling a fib to my father.

A few weeks passed. I had begun having night terrors and had a recurring dream that a giant witch lady was coming to pick me up and scoop me into a basket and take me away. She cooked people on rocks and ate them. I understand how ridiculous this sounds, but it was a chilling and grisly dream that I had often. She was a witch who lived in the woods and would use the souls of her former victims to gather up more children.

It eventually got so bad that I needed to know what was happening. I certainly could not talk to anyone about it and so I prayed to God every night to keep the spirits away, and some nights it worked, and others it did not. I was very sincere and very scared having to go into my bedroom after sunset. There were times when I could not sleep at all, and other times when I would silently cry myself to sleep wishing they would leave me alone. I always knew when they were present because I could feel them in the room with me, and outside my window watching me. The piles of rocks kept appearing near the house during that year, and I would always see shadowy figures out of the corner of my eye after sunset.

A year later, on my 15th birthday, I was having an outdoor picnic with some of the people from the town and a few old friends of my dad's from down south. One of his friends was an American ex-serviceman whom my dad had become close to during the war, and he brought along his friend who was an old Native American Indian we called Long John.

Long John was a real character and to us was a bit of a hero as we had never seen a 'real life Indian' before. As we sat around on the grass eating we hung on his every word. After a while, he said something that made my blood run cold. He told us kids not to wander off too far into the woods and stay close or the giant witch will get us. Stunned, I asked him to repeat what he just said, and sure enough I had heard correctly. He explained that it was an old Native American legend that giant witches lived in woods and would come and steal children away from their parents when they wandered too far. She would heat up rocks and put the children on the rocks and cook them up for supper. I could not believe what I was hearing, and it knocked the wind out of me because it was so close to my own dreamed experiences.

Long John saw my face and asked me what as the matter. After I told him he comforted me and handed me a charm. I started carrying that protective charm around with me, which had been made by one of the elder shaman. He told me that it made me appear in my astral form as a tall and strong hunter to the shadow people and the witch so that they would leave me alone. It may have been a trick of psychology, but whenever I carried that talisman with me, which was a leather bag stuffed with herbs and bark, a bottle cap and an eagle feather tied together, I never was bothered long by these creatures. I simply had to point at them and they would scatter and not return. I still had that same charm up until recently, over 60 years later.

BEWARE OF THE BOGEYMAN SHADOW

When I was 15 I was attacked by a shadow figure while sleeping. I remember it like it was last night. I was sleeping upstairs in my parents' house in Newark, some time in November or December, and often slept with the window opened because it was always hot in my room. For some reason I awoke that night and started hearing voices, more like whispers, coming from outside my window. At first I just thought it was my friends playing a trick, but I soon realised that they were not quite human voices talking to me. Then, out of the corner of my eye, I saw that there were faces hovering at the window. When I tried to look at them directly they simply turned away and disappeared. They kept saying what sounded like 'It's coming! It's coming! Don't let it inside you!'

For some reason I felt that these entities, that were seemingly trying to help, were familiar to me, and somehow I knew what they were talking about.

It was still dark in my room. The street light shined in a little but it was still very dark. I looked at my door and, even through the gloom, could see a very dark shadow, almost smoky in appearance, coming up through the bottom of my door. It did not have a figure at that point, it just slowly rose above me and slid behind me while I was sitting up in bed, frozen to the mattress. I put a pillow over my face because I thought whatever it was was trying to take my body over as its own.

All of a sudden what felt like two arms wrapped around my face with such force it felt like a punch. The pillow I was using to try and stop whatever this thing was from entering my body was now causing me to suffocate. As soon as I thought I was going to die, however, everything stopped, the pillow fell on my lap and I took several large gasps of air. I immediately ran over to turn on the light and shut my window. I looked at the clock, and it was some time between 3 and 4.30 in the morning.

I did not tell anyone because I did not think anyone would believe me. It was not until several years later, when I was visiting home over the holidays from college and drinking with my family, that I said something to my mum about what had happened to me that night. To my surprise, she told me about a few paranormal experiences that had happened to my younger sister, but there had been nothing like I went through.

Another thing that started happening to me shortly after this encounter is that I started feeling strong vibrations in my sleep, almost deafening vibrations, and paralysis, and if I was ever awake late at night I felt like I was being watched in a sinister manner. I would get so angry, not scared that something was watching me. I would curse or walk up to where I thought it was and tell it to leave, but I always got the feeling that whatever it was was laughing in my face – which made me feel helpless.

The strange thing from this whole experience is that since the event I am not the same as I used to be. I constantly find that I have a short temper, feel paranoid and very moody. Furthermore, my best friend growing up, who used to basically live with my family at that house, developed a rare case of respiratory cancer and passed away when we just turned 22. I know this sounds irrelevant, but I have heard that evil entities can harm your health and the health of those close to you – so who knows.

THIRD GENERATION

I am the oldest child in my family, and when we were growing up I got the downstairs bedroom which was on the first floor of our two-story house, and we called it the green room. My two sisters and one brother slept upstairs in the loft conversion.

When I was about 11 years old I woke up in the middle of the night for some unknown reason. My bed was against the wall in the corner and I slept with the door almost all the way open. Upon awakening I saw the figure of a man who was almost as tall as the top of the door. He was in shadow, dark and grey, and had on a black old-fashioned hat so that he reminded me of a Victorian man in a long, black trenchcoat. He was moving very, very slowly towards the edge of the door, heading behind it. I was paralysed with fear, but after a while I thought to myself that it was crazy and that I was seeing things. I needed to go to sleep so I hopped out of bed and ran to the door and slammed it shut, because by that time the figure had moved behind the open door. To my relief there was nothing there, and I totally forgot about what I had seen until many years later. I never even told anyone about it because I thought it was just shadows that I had seen.

During one of our family gatherings probably 10 or 15 years later we started discussing weird things that had happened in our house growing up. My sister started telling a story about a man she saw in the green room one night after I moved out and she got the room. I perked up and listened. I asked her to describe what she saw, what he was wearing, how tall he was and where he was and what he did. To my amazement, it was the same thing I saw. The exact same thing in the exact same spot and doing the same thing, which was just watching and moving very slowly behind the door.

Many years later my daughter stayed the night at her grandma's and slept in the green room. Again we had a family gathering and we discussed weird things because it seems there was always something weird in our house when we were growing up until my mum had the house blessed. My daughter started telling all of us about a man in the green room and what she saw when she awoke in the middle of the night. It was the same thing, wearing the same hat and coat everthing. So, now I know for a fact that I was not seeing shadows at all that night – he was a ghost.

I KNOW WHAT I SAW

I used to live with my family in West Bridgeford. We've lived there for more than four years and three members of my family out of four had reported seeing a shadowy figure passing through the house. The only person who did not ever see the shadow was my dad, who was most of the time working oversees.

I was the first person to see him. It was already dark outside and I was in my room playing on my computer. I was about to go to the toilet and when I got up, a shadow suddenly ran across the corridor passing in front of my door, and it seemed as if it came from my sister's room, which was just next to mine. I knew that the shadow could not have been her, however, since I could hear her typing on her computer from outside her room. I knew it was not my mum since she was downstairs cooking and it could not my dad since he was working oversees again.

The second time it was seen by my mum. It was late at night, and my dad, sister and myself went out for dinner while my mum stayed at home because she had a slight cold. She was sleeping soundly when suddenly for no reason she woke up and sat up in bed. As she sat up, a shadow ran past her and out through the closed door. My mum thought it was just her imagination since she was really tired and had a slight fever, but after what I had encountered I am not so sure.

The third time it was my sister who saw it. That night, my sister was at home alone, so she invited some of her friends home since they lived just a couple of streets away. They stayed until really late, maybe midnight, then they went. While her friends were going, my sister turned and was outside bidding them goodbye. When she turned around she could see a shadow walking down the stairs because the stairs at our old house had a long thin window which goes all the way from top to bottom, so my sister thought that someone had to still come out to leave. When she went in to check, however, there was no one there.

When we finally moved out of the house, something which I was really looking forward to, I told my dad about my experience but he just laughed it off since he learned a little about psychology when he was young. He said that it was impossible that it was a ghost or that it was just my imagination because I read many ghost stories since I am really interested in occult stuff, ghost stories and unnatural events. Seeing that he did not believe me, I told him as well about my sister's and my mum's experiences, and he said that it was just their imagination because they were too tired. But I still know what I saw...

CHAPTER 8
DEMONS

A demon can be described as the following:

1. An evil spirit or devil.
2. A person, habit, obsession, etc., thought of as evil, cruel, or persistently tormenting.

THE DEMON VISITOR

In the summer of 2007 Nottinghamshire was wracked by a big thunderstorm. I was at my grandma's house in Bramcote and we chose to all go out on the porch to watch the storm. The porch was covered so we did not have to worry about the rain. Everyone eventually wanted to go inside but my mum and I really wanted to stay and watch, so we stayed out alone. My mum was cold and asked me to go grab her a fleecy blanket, so I went inside to fetch one.

When I came back I handed her the blanket and sat down. She was unfolding the blanket and covering herself while I looked out into the distance. I saw some type of shadow walking, it looked human but my grandma's property was all fenced off. Then, in a flash of lightning I saw the shadow's face. It had a blood-red face with yellow sharp jagged teeth and black scratches all over its face. Its fingers were long with long black nails at the end of each. It wore a long black robe with the hood up and it looked weathered. He laughed the most wicked laugh I have ever heard and said 'Go to hell, I'm going to kill you.'

I looked at my mum and asked if she saw it, but she said no and sounded confused. I told her we needed to go in the house right away and so she walked inside with me. Whenever I closed my eyes that night I could see its face staring back at me.

Since that night I saw the demon every night. Initially he would be in my dreams but then it progressed so I would see him when I was awake too. In July 2009, we moved to a new home and everything went away for a while, until one night I woke up to that wicked laugh again. I was scared and opened my eyes slowly. There he was, sitting across the room in my reading chair. I turned on the light and he was gone. I then fell back to sleep with the light on. I have not seen him ever since.

I don't know why this demon picked me. But I have faith that God will help me. I have never been someone who believed that paranormal things could happen until this happened to me.

MIRROR DEMON

I am 17 and live in a suburb of Nottingham. I do not want to name it in case any of the readers are from the same area as I do not want them to be scared. I have experienced paranormal things for as long as I can remember, you see, although most of my paranormal contact has been with ghosts.

I lived in a house in the part of town that was historically where pit workers lived. It was pretty old. I do not know the exact year of when it was built but I had many experiences there, although none that really caused me to feel afraid.

My grandparents lived near Mansfield and collected antiques. My grandmother owned a dresser that had belonged to my great-grandmother and had been old even then, being built in the late 1800s. It had a vanity mirror attached and four drawers on the sides and a long drawer in the middle of the top two. It was kept in a room where my grandmother kept her dolls, a room I had never felt at ease in and typically would not stay in alone.

One day, I must have been 11 or 12 years old, my family and I were visiting and she took us up to her room and was offering us whatever things we wanted to keep, because she was wanting to sell some of the antiques in a shop she had opened up in town. I liked the vanity and asked her if I could have it. She told me it was okay with her so my dad loaded it up in his van. I was very excited, and when we got home my dad connected the mirror to the back of the dresser.

As time went on, I started seeing strange things in the mirror, but they were always out of the corner of my eye and I was never able to see what it was exactly. I heard a lot of strange 'popping' sounds at night. I told my parents and they told me it was just my imagination and that the popping was probably just the house settling. I believed them, but in the back of my mind I felt it was something else.

One night, I was lying on my bed, watching TV. It was a bunk bed and my sister slept on the bottom bunk, me on the top. When my program finished I turned the TV off to go to sleep, but maybe five minutes after turning the set off, I heard the 'popping' and what sounded like groaning coming from somewhere in the dark. I looked over to where the sound was coming from and saw a black figure in the mirror of the dresser. Not like a reflection…it was actually in the mirror! I was trembling, but for some reason, maybe fear, maybe fascination, I could not look away. It shifted, and glowing red circles that must of been the eyes were staring at me. I could not move. The figure started scratching at the mirror and there was a sound like glass breaking, only I could see that there was no broken glass. Then, to my horror, the thing strated crawling out of the mirror towards me. The light coming in through the window caught it and I saw that its skin looked extremely bumpy and it had small horns in its head. It had long claws on its feet and hands. He stared at me with an evil, toothy grin and started toward me. I started whimpering, and managed to shut my eyes tight. I started praying and something made me open my eyes. The thing was almost to the bed. I screamed and managed to turn on the TV. The thing let out a weird cry and ran into the wall that separated the room to the bathroom.

My mother ran in, asking if I was okay. I knew if I told her she would not believe me so I told her there was something on TV that scared me. She told me to not watch scary shows and to go to sleep. I nodded but I did not turn the TV off or go back to sleep. I covered the mirror after that.

Strange things started happening from that night on. There was a munching noise always coming from the wall, like something was chewing on the wood. My dad thought there might be damp after the tiles in the bathtub fell off on to my older sister while she was taking a shower one night. He checked but, sure enough, he could not find any sign of it. I did not like that house; I could not stay in it alone.

When I was in senior school, my parents moved my four younger siblings and I to a new house on the opposite side of town. We had the house built on a lot and I was excited. I thought that maybe a new house would stop the terrors. Everything went fine at first, but then we moved the dresser and mirror to the house. I had a thing about mirrors – as was to be expected – and I could not stand looking at them in the dark. My dad had propped the mirror facing out towards the room, with the intention of putting it on the unit the following morning. I got out of bed and went to turn it toward the wall. As I was turning it, however, it got very heavy and I heard a growl. Then I saw the thing in the mirror again. I screamed and dropped it, and it fell the carpet and shattered. I heard demonic giggling coming from everywhere, and as I turned my head this way and that, I heard something whisper in my ear, 'Thanks for releasing us.'

After that, there were certain places in the house that creeped me out that did not used to. I no longer felt safe anywhere. My sister's room, which was next to the room I was in when the mirror broke, was always cold and felt like someone was watching. My parents' bedroom and bathroom were creepy too. The downstairs, the dining room and living room became very eerie. Everywhere I looked I started seeing shadows dashing around outside the house.

One night, I was taking a shower in my parents' bathroom and I heard a door open and cold air rush in. Thinking it was one of my siblings, I did not say anything. Then the lights turned off. 'HEY!' I yelled. The lights came back on. That was when I realised I had locked the door. Suddenly a black figure pounced toward the shower and started beating on the door of the cublicle. I screamed. Slowly, the door started to open and I pulled on the other side to keep it shut. The whole time I was shrieking for my mum and crying. I heard her at the door calling my name, and suddenly the figure disappeared. Trembling, I got out of the shower, grabbed a towel and opened the door for my mum. I told her everything. She rolled her eyes and sighed. 'Alana, you've been watching too many horror movies. There's nothing here. Nobody came in my room. I was watching TV on my bed and I heard you beating the door and screaming. Nothing happened. Finish your shower.' Then she left. I felt so scared I closed it and got back in the shower to finish.

I even slipped into a deep depression after this, as nobody believed me. I was terrified. I could not sleep in the dark and had to have the TV on. I still have these feelings today, and I am still terrified of mirrors in the dark. But what could I do if my own family did not believe me? All I could think of doing was to pray and so I decided to go into every room in the house and say The Lord's Prayer. Thankfully, since doing that there have been no more experiences to report.

TORMENTED BY THE DEVIL

My mother recently told me that when I was five years old I came to her a few times hysterical, saying that Satan had visited me, warning and threatening me to do something bad to my family if I did not stop them from carrying out a particular ritual at our local temple.

A little while afterwards, however, and after we had gone through with our family ceremony, I went outside on a cold, windy night and looked up at the stars and said, punching the sky: 'You can't get me now, Satan!' Immediately after saying this I heard a man's voice, that I thought was God's voice, say to me: 'Don't tempt Satan.' I heard it loud and clear and ran into the house to tell my mum, but I do not think she really believed me and told me not to tell my dad as he would tell me off for talking about such things.

One night, I awoke to see my bed sheet being slowly lifted off me, and I knew that no one was in the room except me and my brother, who I could see was in the bed on the other side of the room. Again I told my mum the next morning but did not tell my dad. This continued for many years, and one time I woke up and saw grey spirits floating around near my ceiling, and another time I woke up to see a female spirit, reading a book, sitting by my bed at the piano in my room. She turned to look at me, and of course I ducked under my covers while my heart felt like it was going to burst out of my chest.

Another time I heard discordant piano music playing, seemingly endlessly, from another room in the house in the middle of the night, and an eerie light came through underneath my door. Another time in the daytime, just after having my lunch, I saw half the body of a boy walk through me.

I am 46 now and even though I have moved away, to this day I will never forget the events that shaped my childhood, when I grew up in Nottingham.

COMING OUT OF THE CLOSET

I recently moved from South Yorkshire to Nottinghamshire and live in a semi-detached house in Netherfield.

One night soon after I had moved in I was doing some laundry. It is a job I hate doing, so I always make sure I stand in exactly the same position so that I can watch television while I do it. I place all the ironed garments on the sofa, before I take them upstairs and put them away in the appropriate places. On this particular night I had just finished ironing and took a large pile of clothes to my own room and placed them on the bed so that I could transfer them to hangers. As I walked into my room I heard a large thumping noise coming from my wardrobe, but I just thought maybe something had fallen off the top shelf inside. When I opened it to check, however, I could see nothing out of place.

I just shrugged it off and hung my clothes up inside the wardrobe before going downstairs to get my son from his playpen and put him to bed in his cot, which was in my room. I read him a story for about 10 minutes before he drifted off to sleep, and then I decided to take a shower in my en-suite.

No sooner had I got undressed when I heard the thumping noise again, but it was louder this time. I went back into my room and opened the wardrobe door, and what I saw still scares the hell out of me.

I saw a solid black human-like thing sitting on my pile of shoeboxes and it did not have a face. It was sitting in a crouched position and its arms were at its sides. I do not know any more details because I slammed the door and grabbed my son and ran downstairs as fast as I could. My son was screaming because I had scared him when I picked him up out of his cot so fast.

I did not know what to do and so I grabbed some clothes that were still on the sofa and ran with my son to a neighbour's house. I did not even stop to put any shoes on.

Thankfully my neighbour was in and when I told him about what I had seen, he grabbed a baseball bat and went into my house to take a look, while I stayed with my son in his.

He was gone about 30 minutes and then returned to tell me that he could not find anything. He had checked my wardrobe, but all that he had seen which he thought was unusual was that the shoe boxes on the bottom of the wardrobe looked as though they had been scorched with flames on their lids.

I was too scared to go back in my house that night so my son and I slept on my neighbour's sofa, before we returned the next day, to find that my house was peaceful and calm, without any sign of the what I had seen the night before.

I could not live with the wardrobe in my house, so I threw it and its contents in my neighbour's skip and replaced it all with new. Thankfully, I have not had any problems since.

DEMON IN MY BROTHER

In the summer of 1995, when I was nine years old, I was playing on the beach in Mablethorpe with my brother, Thomas. He was almost seven years old at the time. I was building sandcastles and he was trying to find sea-shells. He ran up to me, showing me the shells. He wanted me to know 'if they were good enough'. I asked him what they had to be good enough for and he replied that he was going to do something with them later. I told him they were really good, and with that, he walked back to where he was finding shells and kept looking, while I went back to building sandcastles.

Later that day, our mum and dad had told us that it was time for us to get back in the car to go home to Retford. Once we got in the car, I looked over at my brother, who was having a hard time getting his seatbelt buckled. I told him I would help, but he just made this growling sound and told me he could do it himself. He finally got his belt buckled and we were on our way, and I sulked as I liked my role being the helpful big sister.

CHILLING TALES FROM NOTTINGHAMSHIRE

I kept looking over at him, and I kept catching him smiling in an evil way. I told him to stop, that it was making me nervous and put it down to him just being a boy and messing around. He finally stopped, and he started to take out his shells. He turned to me and said 'Are they sharp enough?'

'What do they have to be sharp enough for?' I asked. He replied he needed nice, sharp shells for 'what he was going to do later'. I told him he should not be using sharp things, but he did not seem to take any notice.

When we got back home, my brother asked me if his shells could hurt someone. I told him I would take those shells away if he kept asking me stupid questions. I was beginning to feel very nervous when my brother pretended to be stabbing something or someone and made stabbing noises like a knife plunging into someone's heart or throat. I told him to stop or I would tell Mum and Dad. Thankfully, he stopped for a while.

Then, a few hours later, he started making those slashing sounds again. I told Mum and Dad what he was doing, and they told me to tell them if he did it again and they would do something about it. He did it even more than before, and so I told my parents. They stomped into the room where my brother was and told him to stop what he was doing. He then growled, a sound like nothing I have ever heard from a seven-year-old. It sounded like a demon to me. He marched over to my mum and dad and slashed a very sharp shell at them. I screamed, and my dad caught the hurling shell in his palm – creating a few cuts – right before the shell hit my mother. She was so horrified, that she told the family that we were going to take Thomas to see the priest at the local Catholic church for an exorcism. We sprinkled the house with Holy Water for that night, and let things be.

The next day, we went to visit the priest and he gave the exorcism. After that, my brother was fine. I do not ever think I will ever forget those 'pretending-to-slash-you' moments. It was scarier than anything I have ever seen.

DEMONS TOOK OVER MY LIFE

When I was 16 years old and in the final year of Bramcote secondary school, I became very depressed and felt like I wanted to kill myself. On 13 October 2006, the year after I left school, I tried committing suicide by taking all of my mum's medication. She had about six bottles of different medications and I swallowed all of them. After that I began hallucinating, but thank God my mother found me in time and took me to hospital. The doctors pumped my stomach and said I was very lucky to be alive, as I had swallowed over 100 pills. They kept me in the hospital for a couple of days for observation.

I had been depressed for a while, but I do not know what made me actually want to try to commit suicide. I remember sitting on the bathroom floor and I just felt like something went in me, something really bad, and I just wanted to end my life. But everything really started when I was released from hospital.

The night I was released form the hospital I just expected to go home and relax and sleep, as I was so exhausted. However, for some reason I woke up around 2am and saw the most terrifying thing I have seen in my life. I saw figures all over my wall that looked like demons. I closed my eyes tight and I thought when I opened them nothing would be there. But when I opened them the faces were still there. I did not want to scream because my parents were sleeping and I just thought I was hallucinating. I stayed up the whole night and could not wait for the morning to arrive.

I told my mother and my sisters that I had seen demon faces but they did not believe me, they said I was just tired and stressed and to get some sleep. Which was frustrating, as I know what I saw.

The next night I woke up again in the middle of the night because I was hearing voices in my pillow. Scared, I took the Bible I had in my room and started praying, but the voices just got louder and I felt like I was going crazy. I jumped off my bed, crying hysterically, to my mum's room. She told me she did not hear anything in my room. I asked her to sleep with me in the room and she said yes. My mother went to sleep in the bed with me, and the crazy thing was, as I was lying down, I was still hearing voices. I cried and told her, 'Don't you hear the voices?' and she said 'No'. She held my hand and prayed for me but nothing made the voices go away.

I kept hearing voices in my pillow and I kept seeing the demon faces. Then things started to move around the house on their own, and this my mum witnessed for herself.

I became even more depressed and I even lost weight because I was scared to death. One night I woke up to feel the mattress on my sister's bed starting to rise above the bed on its own while my sister was on it, fast asleep. I froze and I just began praying until eventually I could move, and then I jumped out of my bed and out of the room. My sister woke and screamed and the mattress returned to the bed.

I felt like all of this was happening to me because I tried taking my own life. I begged my mum to get a priest to come and pray for me and she did. When the priest came he started praying for my sister and me. I started seeing the faces on the wall and a black figure. I kept crying to the priest telling him there was a demon bothering me that would not leave me alone, and he told me to close my eyes, not to pay attention to what I was seeing. He told me, 'Have faith in God, he's here with you, and now pray with me.' He kept praying with me until all of a sudden I felt a hot presence run throughout my whole body and then a sudden weakness. I opened my eyes and everything just disappeared, and I could no longer see anything demonic.

I will never forget the experience I went through. I even became more religious because if it. If it was not for the priest, who knows what could have happened to me? I know some of you out there must thing this is a joke but it's not. Demons and evil spirits do exist.

THE DEVIL'S GOING TO GET ME!

I have always been into Halloween and the paranormal, even as a young child. I remember when I first started seeing signs of a possible paranormal encounter when I was about seven or eight years old. My youngest sister would have conversations with someone I could not see. It looked like she was literally talking to the walls. I did not understand, and when my mother and I tried to snap her out of these conversations she would not listen and simply keep talking.

At the time I did not think anything of it. I thought maybe she was at the age where she had created an imaginary friend or something. When I asked her about it, however, she said she had no idea what we were talking about. This continued for at least a year, then it seemed to decrease and slowly stop.

About a year later I was lying in bed, almost asleep, when I felt a hand grab my shoulder. Automatically I got a chill, jumped up and ran for my mum's bedroom. Ever since then, I was afraid to sleep in my room. I know this sounds cheesy, but I had always been afraid of the devil coming into my room. I would scream, cry and have panic attacks because I felt like the devil or something evil was going to possess me. This went on for years, I was terrified.

I started writing horrible, dark lyrics around the age of eight. I had no idea what was going on. My older sister had woken up one morning with scratches all over her back, some of which were in the shape of a cross. I was terrified when I saw this because I knew something was happening when nobody seemed to believe me.

Later that week I had another panic attack. I was terrified that the devil was near so I slept out in the hallway. I was falling asleep when I looked up at the bathroom door and saw a dark, hooded figure. At first I was scared, terrified, but I could not move at all. It seemed like I was frozen. There was no face to it, nor hands and feet. All I could see was the shape of a body, with square shoulders as if it was possibly a man. As I looked up at it, I was puzzled for a moment, then I just simply smiled at it. To this day, I have no idea why I did such an odd thing.

Last year I actually found out that my cousin had seen the same thing in her house; a figure with no face and a hood. Like me, she too was frozen, and for some reason it made her smile. Some people I have discussed it with say it is an evil thing, some say it is not. All I know is that I am terrified that I will encounted it again.

CHAPTER 9
DREAMS AND
NIGHTMARES

A nightmare is often described as a dream that has a negative theme or energy associated to it.

HELL OF A DREAM

I am 26 and often have nightmares, some of which are so vivid and disturbing they stay with me most of the next day. I would like to tell you about a few of the more lucid ones.

One night I had been asleep for a few hours when I either sat up in bed or was dreaming that I did. I was looking straight ahead of me into the corner of my room in front of my wardrobe. Standing there in front of my wardrobe and next to my chest of drawers was a small boy of about the age of six. He was dressed in a navy blue jumper and jeans, he was a little taller than my chest of drawers and had short brown hair. He started to come towards me and reached out his hand towards my face. I recoiled and moved back further up the bed. He stretched forward and touched my chin, which really scared me because I could feel his cold hand pressed against my skin.

With that I screamed at him and leapt forward and pushed him backwards. As I did so I felt him; he felt solid, which shocked me. My push sent him backwards and he hit his head on my chest of drawers, and I distinctly heard the crack! Then, suddenly, he was gone and I realised I was awake, sitting on the edge of my bed with my feet on the floor and my heart pounding. The boy was not there and my husband and children were still fast asleep.

In another dream I dreamt that I was woken by someone saying my name. I looked around the room and at first all I saw was a towel hanging off my bedroom door handle and my chest of drawers with a deodorant spray right on the edge. Then my name was said again, and when I turned to look where it was coming from I saw a man crouching on the footboard of my bed. Behind him the window was open and my curtain was blowing slightly; I noted that I had left the window open because it was a hot summer night.

I watched this 'being' and he watched me. He had long, lank brown hair, a pale complexion and long fingernails. He started to speak to me and I was scared out of my wits. I felt that I should try to befriend him so he would not harm me. While he was speaking I turned to look at my husband and he was sleeping with his back to me, and I thought I could hear him breathing. I sat and listened to the 'being' as he spoke and leered, trying to look as if I did not mind his presence. Then I told him that if he left now, I would promise to leave the window open in future so he could visit and continue the conversation, but I was very tired now. To my relief, he agreed and left.

The next morning I woke up and had forgotten about my dream until I noticed the towel hanging off my door handle, and sure enough the deodorant spray was right on the edge of my chest of drawers! Boy did I get the creeps – was it a dream or not?

FOXY OTHER

When I was about five or so I used to have what I presumed were recurring dreams. However, after I talked to a girl I used to work with I now believe that they may have been memories from a different life.

In one of them I was walking down a lane and a man told me that if I carried on walking I would die. The man looked strangely like 'the Head' on the television show *Art Attack*. He spoke in riddles and some words I did not understand, so I just ignored him and carried on.

I walked until I came to a stream with no bridge, where I would then wake up, every time. The next night I would do exactly the same but there would be, say, half a bridge, then I would wake up. The next time there would be a full bridge, and so on. This carried on for a number of weeks, until in my dreams I reached a big open field. I ran out of a wooded area and then I was shot with a gun and died.

All through the dreams I had been seeing it through someone else's eyes, but now it was as though my spirit was lifted out of my body and gave me a bird's-eye view of the scene. I can still see this scene vividly in my mind. The field was massive and square shaped with little apple trees stationed at regular intervals across it. There was a wooded area that I had just run out of and a small cottage opposite the wood. The man with the gun was walking towards me and I was a fox.

I have read somewhere that in your previous life you can be anything, so once my spiritual teacher said it may have been me remembering. I figured it made sense, because what normal five-year-old would dream of herself as a fox being killed?

LOST LOVE?

One night I was at my boyfriend's house, the moon was full and it was a clear and cloudless night. Danny and I were sleeping, and I was having the strangest dream. I dreamed I was a general and my armies were preparing for battle, when suddenly we were ambushed. I remember striking off the heads of the ambushers, but they had the faces of people I know and love! This dream seemed to be set in a much different time period, yet I was killing my boyfriend, my family and everyone I knew. Then it changed and I saw a man with green eyes and black hair staring at me. Then we were alone and he was holding me, trying to tell me he loved me, and one thing I will always remember about it was that he told me he would see me soon. I saw his green eyes one more time and then I woke up.

It was a bright and sunny day but I felt like something was pulling me down and I felt an overwhelming feeling of power and depression. I was so sad inside that Danny and I started arguing because he said that I was ruining his day with my mood. Furious, I stormed to our bedroom and lay down on our bed and it was not long before I started to cry.

As I lay on the bed feeling very sorry for myself, I felt someone sit down on the bed and start stroking my leg. I thought that it was Danny but did not want to look as I was still mad with him. All of a sudden I went icy cold and sat upright in bed to see that it was not

Danny but it was a ghost of a man sitting on my bed, the same man that I had dreamed about with the green eyes.

I screamed and Danny heard it from the lounge and ran upstairs to see what was the matter with me, but as soon as he entered the room he too saw the ghost and screamed. The ghost then looked at Danny and disappeared.

To this day I have not got a clue who the ghost was or why he showed himself to me in a dream and then to me and Danny, but ever since, when I am in the bedroom on my own, I get the most horrible sense of depression and sadness, like you feel when a relationship has broken up.

COMFORT BLANKET

My name is Livie and I live in Mansfield. I have many ghost stories that have happened to me personally; however, I would like to share one that occurred around three years ago, and one that I believe is very significant from all that I have witnessed.

The majority of experiences occur in my sleep, and it has got to the stage that I now know the difference between a normal dream and a 'surreal' dream. This particular night I went to bed like any other night, and it was in my dreams that I met two men somewhere in a green park, which looked a bit like Wollaton. I walked up to them and sat down on the grass, where they fell silent and studied me. This happened for a little while, and then one of them nodded his head slightly and disappeared.

The other, all of a sudden, was sitting in front of me, and, while still studying me, he began to tell me of his life. He told me that, like he did, I had a lot of hard work ahead of me and that I was never to consider quitting. Throughout this conversation, it seemed like he was looking down at me, like he was rising above me. He then mumbled something, and I looked extra hard at him while asking him to repeat himself.

This is when I realised that my eyes were open and he was sitting cross-legged on the bed right next to me, looking down at me while still speaking. I could see his reflection in the mirror on my cabinet on the other side of him, and to my amazement I realised I was no longer asleep.

The greenness of the park had vanished, and he was now surrounded by the darkness of my room. He had a faint glow and was very lifelike. I tried to look at him closer still, and it was then that he turned his head away from me so that I could not see his face. He sighed, and then I was by myself as he had disappeared.

Unlike other experiences I have had, I was never once afraid. I did feel slightly weird, but I just rolled over and concentrated on sleeping. I believe he could have been lonely or something and needed someone to talk to. But then again, if there is a next time, I hope he stays in my head and keeps out of my reality.

WAS IT A DREAM?

I would like to share a dream/encounter that I had when I was still in college in 1997. This was the year I met my husband.

My brother was in the army and my mum was working a night shift, so I was home all by myself. For the first time in my life I had my own bedroom, because my brother had moved out. We lived in a small semi-detached house, with a kitchen, toilet, dining and living room at the bottom and two bedrooms and a bathroom at the top.

My mum had a dog called Simba and she did not like him to go into her bedroom when she was not there, so I had to go and lock her door with a key as Simba could open doors by jumping up and knocking the handle. I locked the door and went into my own room to watch television, but no sooner had sat down on my bed, when I heard a knocking from inside my mum's locked room. Puzzled, I went to investigate.

I slowly turned the key and pushed open the door, and to my astonishment I saw a little boy spirit sitting on my mum's bed. The little boy looked about four years old, with snow white hair and he looked very sad.

The weird thing was that he kept on calling me 'Mum'. This scared me so much I ran down the stairs to the living room. The child ghost followed me downstairs. I was scared to death, but something came over me and made me feel as if I knew the little boy. A name popped up in my head, which sounded like Jhandry. I do not know why I felt that I knew his name or why I felt as if he was my own.

As the boy approached me his hand reached out to me, as if he wanted me to pick him up and comfort him. I ran past him and I had this feeling of someone grabbing my spine and all my intestines as I passed him. I ran upstairs to my bedroom and locked my bedroom door, pulled my sheets over my head and fell asleep.

The next morning when I woke up, I thought about the previous night and the only explanation was that it must have been a dream.

Years went by but I never forgot the dream. I told my boyfriend, who is now my husband, what happened and he went ice white. He said to me that he had had a son with that name, who had tragically passed away a couple of years before that time. He did not know the boy, and was never informed that the girl he dated at that time was pregnant. They were in the same school together and because she was of Indian origin and he was white, her family didn't approve, so they lost contact.

A year later she came to visit him and introduced him to his son, she did not want anything from him but she felt that it was only fair to let him know that he had a son. Sadly, he passed away that same year. It was to be the first and last time that my husband saw him. We met later that year and got married. My husband showed me a photo of the boy, and the boy in the photo looked similar to the one in my dream, but the photo was not very clear.

I would love to know if it was a dream or a lost boy looking for comfort?

I AM AFRAID TO FIND LAURA

I am 47 years old and I have spent most of my life living in Nottingham. I have always been a vivid dreamer, but two which occurred a few years ago changed my whole view of dreams, and even now I give these two dreams a tremendous amount of thought.

I live in a terrace house and I had been helping my neighbour Ben since early mending the garden fence that separated our two gardens. It was snowing and as more was forecast we had decided that we had better fix it before it got any worse.

After we had finished Ben and I had a few beers and then I wandered slowly home. The next day I had my own work to do, restoring an old motorcycle. The engine was almost finished and I was really looking forward to hearing the big old bike come back to life after spending more that 30 years lying unloved in someone's shed.

I was tired and soon I was relaxing in bed. I felt something in the room was not quite right, not as it should be. I was trying to figure out what it might be when I must have drifted off to sleep. It was a deep sleep for when I awoke I had to shake the stiffness from my bones to rise myself in the bed. I could tell too that I was having one of my occasional 'half waking dreams'. The first time had been frightening – by now they had become fascinating.

With half-closed eyes I could see human shapes moving about the darkened room. This was usual, but I would always tell myself in the morning that I had simply imagined these shapes, they were products of my imagination. As I blinked around the room like a drunk in a pub strange things began to happen. The dark mists that floated across the room began to part in the middle and slowly a figure approached my bed. I had never seen any details on the faces of the others who visited in these strange dreams, but now a young girl of about 20 wearing a summer dress approached my bed. Slowly she brought her hands from behind her back, holding a little bunch of spring flowers. She sat on the edge of the bed and took my hand in hers, held it for a few minutes and then got up and walked slowly into the mist, which was now swirling, and was gone. I snatched like a mad man for the light switch and there I lay, a sweating wreck after a silly dream. That dream bothered me for most of the next day but by evening it was slipping to the back of my mind.

The day passed as before, cold and snowy, and I could only do limited work on the bike due to the weather. That night I began to make the bed, and it was while I was throwing an extra bedspread on it and spreading it around to make it more comfortable that something falling to the floor caught my eye. It looked like a moth of some kind, but as I looked closer I saw that it was the head of a little freshly plucked wildflower. There was no way that they were in bloom so early in the year but this one could have been plucked that very day. Where in God's name had it come from? I thought, of course, of the girl in my dream but this made no sense…somehow this flower had found its way into my room. I had no explanation of how it got there. I pressed the flower in the old family Bible, where it still is today, and got on with life.

Finally the spring did come, almost overnight it seemed, and then followed a scorching summer. The sun was unbearable during the day and trying to sleep at night was like simply rolling over and over in sweat. My last encounter took place one night towards the end of August, when the warm spell was at its hottest and rumours of a break in the weather were everywhere. I finally slept, but when I woke up and looked around I was in a whole different place. It was still night, but I was frozen, colder than I had ever been before.

The girl from my last dream was sat beside me with her full winter outfit on, her hand linked under my arm. In front of us was a frozen pond where children were skating and laughing, although I could tell by the moon that it was well after midnight. I knew I was dreaming, but it had never been so vivid before. Had I died and gone here? I tried to ask the girl her name or where we were but the sound would simply not come out. She turned to me and said 'Wasn't the music recital great last night?' I could not answer and next she hauled me by the arm and we walked along a little snowy path. I could barely move with the cold and then an old couple passed us on the path. The man lifted his hat and said 'Laura' and the lady just smiled politely. Neither looked at me.

'Laura' had let my hand go and she was now a little ahead of me, seemingly unaffected by the intense cold. She moved along the edge of the pond where thick mist was now beginning to rise. I tried to follow but the cold had frozen my very bones. I fell to my knees and in an instant I was lying on my bedroom floor, frozen to the bone, in the middle of an August heat wave.

That was seven years ago now, and while I still do not believe in ghosts or spirits, I do give some credence to the possibility of there being other places which we can visit from time to time. Maybe there is some way of reaching these other places through the power of dreams. And there is always the possibility that Laura was not in my dreams...maybe I was in hers?

Anytime I feel like I am on a fool's errand, I open the old Bible and look on that pressed spring flower, a flower that now I am sure came from a girl who either entered my dream, or I somehow entered hers.

SOUL NIGHT

When I was 19 years old I was a student studying at Nottingham Trent University. I am not very religious and consider myself a rational, intelligent person. That being said, I have no explanation for the events I encountered back then.

I was enjoying a normal dream one night, I cannot remember what I was dreaming of, when at some point my subconscious abruptly shifted into a nightmare. I remember that was strange, as for some reason I can usually tell when I will have a nightmare as I can feel a fear growing inside and pretty much know it is my own unrest and anxiety that provokes them; however, this time was different.

In my dream I took on a first-person view of my surroundings. I was standing on concrete, which had cracks and potholes littering its surface. Around me a sea of black threatened to engulf the island of concrete I was standing on.

My view then changed to a third-person perspective where I could no longer see myself but rather a gigantic muscular demon, who now stood on the other side of the concrete island. It felt very much that we were going to engage in some sort of fight and I felt almost eager to match myself against this thing. A battle of wills started.

At first I was holding my own against this monster but inexorably it pushed on me and I could feel my mentality and spirit weaken. Once I realized I could not win against it I was terrified. I knew that if I gave up I would be consumed, not only in the dream but somehow crossing into reality; damnation awaited me and I would never wake up. In desperation I started reciting the Lord's Prayer out loud to this monster. I felt electrified. An incredible feeling of power and complete bliss devoid of any fear filled me. I pushed back against the demon, crushing it utterly and completely. Then I woke up.

I lay in my bed with the covers over my head, letting my warm breath heat my cloth cocoon. I lay there, fully awake, for a good 10 minutes contemplating my dream when I felt a crushing weight cover my body and press me into the mattress. I could not breathe and was terrified. I instinctively knew this was related to the dream I had. Then the demon from my nightmare whispered in my ear in a slow menacing voice, 'God is dead...'

After that the weight I felt lifted off my body. I was in shock over experiencing this event while awake, as I had at first reasoned to myself that it was only a dream. I try to stay logical about this, as it could have been just a bad dream, sleep paralysis and the over-active imagination of a young man. What I believe in my heart, however, is that I fought a demon for my soul.

RECURRING DREAM

I have had a recurring dream my entire life involving 'the dark man'. I may sound crazy, but something about this dream is different than any other dream I have. I am starting to think there is something to it and I would like to know if it strikes a chord with anyone else.

For the past 26 years I have lived quite near to Sherwood Forest, and at night it is dark and quiet; the only light is the streetlight in the driveway. All of my life I have had an inexplicable fear of the back corner of our property – something down there scares the hell out of me. In my recurring dream, it is nighttime and I am in the driveway under the streetlight. I am alone and it is completely quiet except for the sound of the odd owl hooting in the distance. At first there is no wind and it is muggy and hot. But then, from the back of the property comes a howl like a wolf. The wind picks up fiercely. Then, I know this is bizarre, but a man dressed like a Tibetan monk grabs my shoulder and says the following verbatim: 'He is coming, but do not fear him. If you do, his eyes will take you.' He then returns to a circle of men in monks' clothes and joins in a weird chant with them. Then I look back towards the woods and a black wind sweeps through the trees. The monks chant louder and he appears. The best way I can describe him is that the wind took the form of a man with some sort of wide-brimmed hat.

Two things I should mention is that he seemed to have no form at all, just a shade or something; a kind of smoke, but shaped like a man. He was more than just dark. It is like he was a walking black hole or something. The other thing was his eyes. He never speaks, he just drifts up to me. Face to face. And his eyes are burning red. He just stares into my eyes, and even though I cannot make out a mouth, he seems to be smiling.

Just then I hear a baby screaming and he vanishes. And that is when I awake.

There are other dreams I have about him, but that is always the basis of my experience. Always there is a child, and always there are people dressed as monks chanting. I have never been a fanatic for premonitions or dream phenomenon, but I am starting to think there is something to this thing.

The 'dark man' has tormented my dreams my entire life. I thought I was crazy, but I have been told too many accounts of him from other people that seemed to match my own a little too closely.

Anyone who knows me knows that I am a very logical guy. I search for physical proof and scientific explanation, but these dreams seem so real it is as if they are actually happening. No sleep paralysis, just the dark man. Darker than dark. As if he were a walking black hole of light and matter.

CHAPTER 10
HAUNTED
HOUSES

A house which is described as haunted is believed to have experiences of supernatural occurrences or paranormal phenomena. A haunted house may contain ghosts, poltergeists, or even malevolent entities such as demons.

Haunted houses are often perceived as being inhabited by disembodied spirits of the deceased who may have been former residents or were familiar with the property. Supernatural activity inside homes is usually thought to be associated with violent or tragic events in the building's past such as murder or death.

It is interesting to note that the statistic gathering company Gallup conducted a poll in 2005 in three countries – the United States, Canada and Great Britain – to gain a greater understanding of people's opinions on the subject from different walks of life and genres. The findings showed that more people believe in haunted houses than any of the other paranormal items tested, with 37 per cent of Americans, 28 per cent of Canadians and 40 per cent of British people believing.

HAUNTED HOUSE

I used to own a home in Aspley, which was built in 1905 and had a gravel driveway. My older stepson Erik used to practice witchcraft, although my husband and I would argue over Erik doing this worship in our home. My husband told me that Erik was just going through a teenage phase, but I disagreed and had a strong feeling that things were not right.

You see, ever since Erik started practising witchcraft in our home we have started experiencing paranormal occurrences. I was working a lot of hours at a recruitment agency in Nottingham and so was usually very stressed, but when I would fall asleep at home, I would have strange dreams. For example, I dreamt I saw the devil flying through my home, and demons too.

Then, in other dreams, I dreamt that the mortgage papers were being ripped up. I even saw the house falling down. My imagination was running away with me and it was starting to have an impact on my waking hours as I was so tired all the time. I started to argue with Erik over his practices, which was a shame as we had always been close.

One day after rowing with Erik about the fact that all the dishes were going missing, he stormed out of the house, and because I had a feeling that they were all under his bed, probably with mouldy food on, I decided to venture into his bedroom.

I opened his bedroom door and what I saw really disturbed me. In the middle of the room was a demonic Bible and there were candles set out in a circle. I was alarmed that Erik was so deep into witchcraft. I retrieved my dishes, shut the door tightly and waited downstairs for my husband to return from work so we could discuss what to do about Erik.

When my husband came home, Erik was still out, so we both ventured upstairs into his room. No sooner had we opened the door, when all the books on his shelf started to fly at us, like something out of a horror movie. My husband started swearing, not understanding what was going on, as more things were thrown at us by this unknown force.

My husband grabbed the Satanic Bible, and ran downstairs and out into the garden. He then set fire to it with a match and we heard a piercing scream as the book set on fire.

When Erik came home, we told him what we had witnessed and he said that he too had witnessed things in that room but had become too scared to move the book or the candles. He promised never to dabble in anything like that again and he has been true to his word. Thankfully, we have never experienced anything like it since.

FOOTSTEPS

I have lived in my house for a little over a year now, and nothing paranormal has happened, until recently.

It was a Saturday, not too long ago, and it was 12:30 am. I was the only one awake in the house; everybody else was asleep. I was on my computer in my bedroom when I heard a noise, like a TV being turned on. I thought it was just someone in the family who could not sleep and had decided to watch TV, so I did not worry about it. I continued on the computer until about 1:00 am, when I decided I wanted to go to sleep. I walked out of my room, because

I had to use the bathroom, and I saw that the TV was not on after all, and everybody was obviously still in bed. But the noise was still there. It was loud, and I was surprised that it had not woken anybody up yet. I walked into the living room to find it pitch black, but that the radio was on. I was a little freaked out, so woke up my parents to tell them about it. My dad got up and turned it off for me. I asked how it turned on by itself, and he said that my little sister, who is two years old, likes to play with it and must have accidentally set an alarm. I was not convinced, because the only radio we had was high up, and there was no way my little sister could reach it; I can barely reach it myself. I was puzzeld, and had no explanation for what had happened.

I went to the bathroom, left the door open because there is a night light in there, and went to bed. When I was in bed, about five minutes later, I heard a creaking noise. I knew it could not be someone walking around, since we have tile floors and they do not creak. I sat up, and looked through the crack of my open door. I watched in fear as the bathroom door started to close itself, with nobody pushing it shut. The door did not shut completely, but it got halfway there. I calmed myself down, and went back to bed. Then I heard the creaking noise again, and saw the bathroom door being pulled open now. I sat there, staring at it for a few minutes, but nothing else happened.

When I woke up the next morning I tried to process in my mind what I had seen. The radio must have come on by itself, because there were no other explanations. I looked at the bathroom door, but I could find no reason for it opening and closing by itself.

I now believe in ghosts. I think my house is haunted, even though I do not have much evidence. I can just feel it; I feel like I am being watched. I feel as though there is a spirit just looking for attention, or trying to make itself known.

About a week later I was in my bed, all by myself, when I heard footsteps outside of my room. I sat up, and waited for a minute. The footsteps continued coming own the hallway, and I heard them stop in front of my door. I then heard a scrape against my door, like someone was reaching through to open the door handle. A minute later, as I quivered with fright beneath my covers, I heard footsteps in my room. They sounded like they were coming to me. I eventually built up the courage to say 'Go away' to the ghost and the sound of footsteps stopped. Slowly, I looked out from my duvet, and whatever it was had gone – for now.

BHANAMATI POSSED

I am not sure what the exact translation of the word 'poltergeist' is in the Hindi language. But in one of my native Indian languages there is a term called *bhanamati*, which is almost the same but used in much wider perspective. The chain of events that I am going to narrate can be loosely related to the same term. Before I heard about the incidents and got involved, the situation had already become quite serious and was drawing a lot of attention.

The first incident took place in the bedroom of Mohan, who is 28 years old. Mohan was standing in front of the mirror, applying face cream before retiring for the day. In the mirror, he saw a sudden and fast movement behind his head. He ducked instinctively, only to see a small copper pot crashing into the wall near the mirror. It had missed the back of Mohan's head and the mirror by couple of inches.

Mohan was not afraid because he did not understand the significance of what had happened. At first he thought someone had thrown the pot at him, but there was no child in the house who possibly could have done this kind of mischief. His parents rushed to the room because of the noise. Mohan refrained from going into details because he thought his parents would worry unnecessarily. He was intentionally vague about what happened and when his parents left he placed the pot where it was. It was a heavy and richly decorated copper pot. Mohan had bought it from an antique fair in Newark. It was quite costly and must have been poured around 120 years back, and for some reason Mohan had been strangely drawn to it and considered it an investment.

Exactly the same thing happened four days later, but this time the showpiece flew at him when Mohan was coming towards his bed. The piece hit him squarely under the right ear and opened up a cut, which bled quite profusely and required two stitches. This pressed the panic button in the family and the word got around in the community that something abnormal was happening in the house. The copper piece was kept under lock and key in the kitchen cabinet after that, safely tucked away under heavy utensils.

I came to know about the incidents in July 2001. By that time there were a few more scares, out of which two were notable. The first one took place late evening when Mohan had just come back from work. His mother had brought family jewellery from their bank safe because she wanted to wear it during a marriage ceremony the next day.

The ornaments were kept in a small but very compact wooden box of sandalwood, which was a family heirloom. This box was kept on a table in the hall. The moment Mohan entered the house this box flew from its place and hit him in the stomach. It was a nasty blow and Mohan was lucky to escape with just a flesh wound and without any serious internal injury. On another occasion, when the family was having their dinner together in the kitchen instead of dining table, the copper pot moved again. There was a great force behind the movement which made the utensils on top of the pot become dislodged, and the wooden cabinet door almost came apart. The 'evil' cube and pot were then moved to a neighbour's house.

It was quite tough to get entry into the house and win confidence of the family. I had a friend in the community who used to know Mohan's cousin. With her acquaintance, we could meet Mohan and start understanding the problem. The news of these accidents had already spread in the nearby communities and there was a good probability that it would have hit the media as well, if it leaked out. Already one or two self-proclaimed researchers had tried providing unfounded and incorrect scientific explanations.

One thing struck me straight way. Each incident had taken place when Mohan came back from work and every time he had reached home late. Also, all the objects that were hurled towards him by whatever power that was driving this were very old. Since the family was not ready to let me bring these artifacts in the house I went to the neighbour's place to take a look.

Both the copper pots and the wooden cube must have easily been more than 100 years old. There was a connection somewhere. My friend was of the opinion that the root cause of the problem was outside the house and not inside. I agreed to his hunch because there was no permanent 'feeling' in the house, which generally accompanies haunted places.

When I asked Mohan what he did for living he told me that he was a civil engineer with good aptitude for interior decoration. After doing a salaried job for a year or so, he had quit and started his own business. Right now he was working on four sites and his business was seen as one of the smaller but promising upcoming firms. He was not able to remember anything specific he had done on his sites when he was attacked, but one very significant fact came out of our discussions.

One of his sites was almost on the outskirts on the city. Whenever he went there he came back home very late because the commuting itself took around two hours in one direction. He also mentioned that the particular work was not going well and he was under pressure to complete it. Quite surprisingly, Mohan himself seemed to have given some thought to the matter and admitted that he had once felt that the work site might be related to the recent strange events in his life. When we pushed a bit he admitted that he always felt depressed and less dynamic when working on that particular construction.

We decided to visit the site. It turned out to be a spacious three-storey building, which must have been constructed some time in the early 1960s. Oddly enough, the previous construction itself was not completely new, it was more of a renovation, an enhancement and damage repair work for the structure that already existed there. Even the work which Mohan was involved in was not aimed at making any radical changes to the building.

We had a look around the property, and when we climbed the stairs of the second floor we sensed something was wrong. The feeling increased when we reached the third floor. The influence could be narrowed down towards a certain corner of the loft. It was very dusty and getting into the loft itself was quite difficult. We paid one construction worker to throw down whatever was up there. There were few very old utensils and soiled home-stitched clothes made for an infant. The feeling of a presence of an unnatural influence had become so strong that at one point I felt we had made a mistake in coming to this place in the twilight hours. We touched each and every utensil. They were rusty and wasted since they had been lying unused for ages, but they were 'safe'. But when my friend touched the infant clothes he withdrew his hand immediately. When I tried to touch one of the clothes I also felt a very cold shiver running down my spine. There was something nasty attached to the clothes. We still managed to put everything in one sack and pushed it to a corner. In my experience changing the place of a possessed object can help at times because certain associations that have been built are broken.

But we took no further steps. Burning the clothes would have been an option but that would possibly have meant antagonizing the power attached to them. It could have possibly resulted in its release from the clothes and may have created more damage. There was definitely some sad event that must have taken place with the infant for whom the clothes were stitched. But it was impossible to find out what it must have been because all this must have happened almost a century ago.

Apart from Mohan, no one else had suffered. I have often observed that the impact of occult rage varies a lot from person to person. There was something in Mohan that made him the easy prey to the attacks.

We recommend a cleansing ceremony in Mohan's house and advised him to give up the work, which was fetching him very little profit in the first place. Incredibly, the accidents stopped immediately after Mohan's firm stoppd work on the site.

THE VISITORS

I have wanted to believe in ghosts for such a long time, but the older you get I think the more proof you need to believe in the paranormal. My waiting was made worthwhile, however, when I had the proof that I had been waiting for all my life.

About four years ago we moved house to Retford. I thought the new place was great and still do; I never thought it was creepy or that anyone other than our family lived there.

Soon after moving in, however, I started to get an odd feel from the place. Like when you are sure someone's there but you can just never quite catch a glimpse of them. This lasted for about a year or so, at about which time I heard the voices for the first time. About lunchtime one day I came out of my room into the hallway and heard an unknown voice say 'Ian! Over here, come over here…Ian.' I was scared to my core. I ran downstairs, but I never told anyone, I guess I was worried that they would think I was mad.

After it had happened a few times, I decided to tell my mum. She did not think I was mad; in fact she believed me completely, as apparently in our old houses there had been similar things happening. In our last house, for example, my mum and dad had seen a white woman in the mirrors and a black figure who stood on the stairs. She told me that in the house where I was born, things started happening just after they brought me back from the hospital. My bedroom door had slammed shut when all the windows were shut, our cat started acting really weird and staring at empty spaces in the rooms, and my mum would tell my dad that she had seen dark shadows in the corners. He never believed her though, as he does not believe in ghosts or anything like that and has a far more practical mind.

In March 2009, very early in the morning, I saw a ghost. I woke suddenly and for some reason, which I still cannot explain, I turned towards my door. It was open only a couple of inches but through that gap I saw a little boy, the same little boy I had previously seen at the end of my bed but shaken away as a play of the lights. He just walked past. He wore jeans and a blue jumper, had a dark blond mop of hair and quite fair skin, and he was not dressed in old-fashioned clothes as you expect ghosts to be in but more of a 1970s style. Oddly I was not scared, but I was really shocked, and thinking back now I wish I had got up to investigate more. When I told my mum she seemed to doubt me, I am not sure why, maybe because I was not scared and did not wake her up, but her doubt just made me more determined to believe.

I had my next sighting a few months later. These months had been spent watching to see the little boy again; however it was not him who woke me early one morning soon afterwards. I got the feeling that someone was watching me, so I woke up and I was not too surprised to see a white woman sitting at the end of my bed, looking at me. I woke, saw her, blinked, she was still there, blinked again and she was gone. She was completely white except for her short black hair. The funny thing is, she almost looked like my mum when she was younger and seemed to be wearing her white dressing gown.

BREATHING IN BASFORD

The first house I lived in had many inexplicable happenings which led to me believing in ghosts. One night, when I was about eight or nine, I heard breathing and so I went closer to the garage door to investigate. As I did so the breathing grew louder, but when I passed it, it grew fainter. I thought that maybe it was an intruder inside our garage, so I went and told my dad that I heard breathing in the garage and grabbed a baseball bat, my dad grabbed a hockey stick, and we both nervously turned on the light to the garage, but no one was there.

I apologised to my dad but swore that I had heard the noise, and he told me 'Better safe than sorry' and went to sleep. While I was awake in my bed, however, I could still hear the strange sound of breathing, only this time it was coming from near the basement stairs.

From then on, I have believed in ghosts. One night my friend Steve came over and I was telling him of my weird encounter with a ghost, at which point we both heard the breathing coming from the kitchen.

Since we were both in the hallway, we went up the stairs that led us to the kitchen, and as I looked over at my friend I saw that he was shaking.

We stood in the kitchen for a while, listening to the breathing, when Steve started to sneak away and go into the other room. I told him to wait for me, and then as I was about to leave turned and said, 'Hey ghost, why don't you come down and party with us?' At which point all the cups in the cupboard started shaking and clinking, and we both ran out as fast as we could, terrified. The whole night Steve was waking me up saying, 'Did you hear that?' But by then I was used to the breathing sound and it did not bother me.

My family and I owned a really cheap tea party table with four metal chairs, and every once in a while, when the chairs were stacked up on the table, the top chair would fall off. None of the others fell, only the top one. Another night, Steve came over and we heard one of the chairs fall off and bang down the steps in the kitchen. We were in the living room and we both grabbed baseball bats and went to investigate. Steve and I stood there like statues for ages, but saw nothing more.

Even at the house I live in now I have seen some pretty weird things. About 2 o'clock in the morning I will hear the shampoo bottles crash down onto the shower floor. My daughters say that when they are home alone they hear footsteps upstairs and the radio turns on and off randomly. I completely believe them, half because of my childhood and half because they are usually crying their eyes out when my wife and I come home!

I TOLD YOU I WAS ILL!

I had only heard about poltergeists a few times before, mostly in movies like *Beetlejuice* and such, but I had my first real experience about a year ago.

I had moved up into my sister's room when she moved out. It was a large room and we had only lived in the house for about a year. The owners that lived in the house before us had told us that it was used as a clinic many years ago, which was easy to believe because we always found apothecary bottles, tubes and suchlike outside in the garden.

My whole family believed in ghosts but I had never encountered anything until I moved into my sister's old room. I had finally arranged everything the way I wanted it. The access to the attic was in my room, and it had a tendency to open by itself so I had put a big dresser in front of the door that I could barely slide across the floor myself, let alone pick up.

One day my friend wanted me to go to her house for the weekend, so I packed up a few things and left with my mum. My step-dad was downstairs in the living room, which is directly under my room, having arrived home from work a few minutes after we had left. He thought that my mum was still at work and that I was upstairs in my room as usual. He started to hear footsteps in the hallway towards my bedroom, then my door push open and footsteps that sounded like they were going into my room. There followed a few seconds of silence and then a huge thump. He called for me to be quiet but of course I did not answer because I was not there.

When I got home he gave me a weird look. I asked him what was wrong and he told me everything that had happened. I walked up into my room with him behind me because I did not want to go into my room alone if someone was in there. When I walked in I was in shock. My dresser, that was already 80lbs with an extra 30lbs on it from all my stuff, had been knocked down. My things were strewn across my floor and the attic door was wide open against the wall. I cleaned everything up and told myself that I was not going to let the strange event scare me off. But then things started to get worse.

I started having pain in my dreams that felt completely real, which I know is not abnormal, but I started to wake up with cuts, bloody noses and scratches on my arms. I would find blood on my walls and smeared on my windows. Not like in the movies where it is drenched, they were just small spots, but blood is blood. I started to become depressed and cry a lot whenever I was in my room. I had feelings of wanting to hurt myself and other people. I began to have harmful images run through my head, yet I never wanted to leave the room or be outside. I hated everything in the world that I once loved and began to starve myself for no apparent reason. After some time, I knew that I needed to get out of the room for good.

I switched rooms with my mother and my step-dad, who did not think the room was the reason for my problems. I had always had a tendency to sleepwalk and move in my sleep, and my mother thought I had hurt myself by accident while sleepwalking. A few weeks passed with her being in that room when she finally began to become depressed too. It was a slow start at first but she began to fall into a depression and cried a lot. My step-dad felt weird vibes about being in the room alone and never wanted to go near the wardrobe. He was unable to sleep and soon my mum found herself the same way. It eventually led to her staying downstairs and never going to her bedroom, until she feels as though she will pass out if she does not sleep.

My step-dad had no choice but to call a medium, who came to the house and cleansed it from top to bottom. She told us that there was a spirit of a woman in the room, who the doctors were unable to help as they thought that she was a hypochondriac but she was really ill and died. We all prayed for her, and since that day there have been no other problems.

HOUSE FILLED WITH SHADOWS

I am 17 years old, and since I was nine I have seen and felt peculiar things in my house. My mum had experienced paranormal phenomenon during her life so it annoys me when she says it is just my imagination. But my friend tells me that her mum does the same thing and that she is just trying not to scare me more.

I have always felt eerie things in my house. My female dog sometimes barks at certain places in the house, usually in the kitchen and at the stairs, but no one is ever there. I saw someone in the kitchen once but I thought I imagined it because when I turned around to check, there was nobody about. Sometimes I go downstairs and my dog is sitting in front of the stairs in the living room looking at them, and she seems relieved when she sees me. When I try to get her back into the kitchen where she should be, she refuses to go. She usually listens to me, so it scares me when she acts like this. Other times she sits in a corner far from the kitchen and if I call her she does not move, she just looks at me, and if I go near her she seems happy. That is also weird because she always comes to me when I call her so I can tell there is something wrong. I once took a photo of the stairs and I could clearly see a figure sitting on them.

My mum has fallen from those stairs a million times, my dog refuses to climb up them, and my friend feels like someone will try to push her off every time she climbs them.

Once, during the summer, I was having a weird dream. In my dream, I woke up lying on the right-hand side of my bed, my body facing the wall but my eyes looking at the door in front of the bed. It was dark, and there were noises. I wanted them to stop but they did not. Suddenly a woman in a white dress passed right in front of my door. I was terrified, wishing she would not come inside the room. I screamed at her to 'Go away' and thankfully she did.

I have not seen any more ghosts and I hope that I never do. However, if you see one, just be assertive and tell them to 'Go'.

CHAPTER 11
IMAGINARY FRIEND OR FOE?

An imaginary friend is often described as a spirit which befriends and builds up a relationship with a living person. The living person is often able to describe key features and traits about the 'friend' even though other people are unable to see or witness them.

ROSIE

This story happened years ago, when I lived in Bulwell with my family. I cannot remember the exact age, but I think I was probably about 10 years old.

Years before I was born, when my grandma was only 10 or so, she had a cousin named Rosie. Rosie died from cancer around the age of 11 or 12 and my grandma was devastated; she still gets upset now if I mention her.

Growing up I was always fascinated ghosts and sprits. I used to see them everywhere. I never had many friends, but one of the ghosts that I saw was a girl who I called Rosie. She was there all my life. My dad once told me I was talking about her as soon as I could speak. I loved Rosie but because the rest of my family could not she her they just said I was making it all up. Except for my dad, of course, who always believed me and said he could feel her presence too.

What started bothering my mum and grandma was when I started drawing pictures of Rosie. In my pictures I drew her how I saw her. She had lovely brown eyes with beautiful long brown curly hair. There was always a big bow in it and she always wore an old-fashioned green dress with flowers all over it.

One day my mum and I were cleaning out my grandma's house. We found a bunch of jewellery boxes stuffed with precious necklaces and bracelets. My curiosity got the better of me and I had to have a look in them. I found a gorgeous locket that was wrapped up the most. I showed it to my grandma but she burst into tears when I showed her. My mum finally explained to me because I could not understand.

We took the necklace home. My mum got out the pictures I drew. Inside the locket was a picture of my grandma's cousin. The face on my drawing and the face on the photo were the same. We think that Rosie saw that I could see ghosts and looked after me, because my parents argued a lot and it upset me.

Soon my mum and dad were fighting for custody for me and I got depressed. Rosie helped me through it all and I started to get better. But Rosie started fading away. So did all the other ghosts. Now I can only feel them and see them from the corners of my eyes. I never wanted Rosie to leave and I never understood why she did.

YOU'RE MINE

My first experience with the paranormal was at my grandparents' house in Lenton. I was very close with them, so from the age of six years old I would spend just about every other weekend with them. It seemed that only when I was there I had an imaginary friend named Debbie. There were many children my age that lived on their street, even a schoolmate of mine, so my family could not understand why I would create a friend.

Debbie was not a figment of my imagination. Debbie was older than me, she was a pretty girl with blonde hair. I liked her; she let me pick the games but would get angry if I ignored her. I still remember a time that I had brought my friend Dean to spend the weekend with me at my grandparents' house. I brought Dean to my room and immediately saw Debbie standing in the corner.

Later in the night we were getting ready for bed and Dean went into the bathroom and left me alone in the room. We each had a glass of water on the bedside cabinet, I saw a flash of light and the next thing I knew both water glasses were on the floor and water was all over the rug. My Nana asked how it happened and I told her I did not know. I was across the room when it happened.

In the middle of the night I woke up to Dean shaking me and asking me who was talking. At first I did not hear anything but then I heard a faint voice coming from down the hallway. We were both too scared to get out of bed so I called for my Nana. We told her what happened and she said we were dreaming and to go back to sleep. We knew better, we knew it was Debbie, and she was not happy that Dean was there. I had seen Debbie numerous times after that but never really wanted to bring any of my friends there.

When I got older I overheard my Nana telling my Mum a story about a man who would comfort her when she got upset. Apparently Debbie was not the only spirit in their house!

MY IMAGINARY FRIEND

I am 27 years old, and all of my life I have been tied into the supernatural one way or another. As a child, my mother was a practising witch and I used to have horrible visions, like dreams about people I had never met.

As I grew I began to practise witchcraft on my own, until I became pregnant with my daughter. Due to things I had experienced as a child I did not want to put her in harm's way at all.

My husband and I moved into our house in Warsop almost a year ago, and since moving in I have not noticed any strange vibes or unexplained occurrences; however, over the past few weeks I have noticed my little girl has been acting a bit strange. First I should add that our daughter has a speech delay and does not fully talk. She can say words and sometimes put two words together, but she is in therapy to help with her speech. That being said, I have noticed her in her room having 'conversations' with someone. She looks at them and waits in between her babble as if she is having a normal conversation. My husband believes she just has an imaginary friend, but I think it is more than that. I once saw her imitating facial expressions and actions that she never has done before, as well as opening and closing doors as if letting someone in or out.

The other night, after I put her to bed, I was in the study and I could hear her laughing. I got up to check on her and I saw her wiggling around on the bed as if she were being tickled and giggling like crazy. Once I turned her light on, it stopped. I am a bit concerned, since she cannot talk and tell me what she sees or if it is an imaginary friend. Since my mother has some background in this sort of thing, I told her what had been happening. She then told me a story of my own 'imaginary friend' I had when I was three years old.

Her name was Bea, and I described her to my mother as an elderly woman, and gave great details as to her appearance. My mother then told me that she showed me a photograph of my great-grandmother and asked if that was her, and I said that it was.

My great-grandmother Bea had passed away almost six years before I was born. So I do believe my daughter could be seeing a ghost, and building up a friendship with one. Could Bea be watching over my daughter like she did me?

ROOM FOR ONE MORE?

I am a 31-year-old mother of three. In 1999 I had my first son, and when he was about two and a half years old we moved to Clipstone.

After a while of living in our second-floor flat, my son started to play and talk to an imaginary friend. He called his friend 'Rolly'. We did not think too much about it because we thought it was normal, especially as he was an only child. After some time our son began to include his friend in all of our activities.

When we would travel to see relatives, my son would take his 'friend' with us and did not want us to place anything on the spot that Rolly was sitting at. He would take him to the shops, and everywhere we went Rolly would go too.

One day my son started calling me with fear in his voice and he told me that Rolly had fallen from the balcony. I was surprised and began to think that maybe his friend was not so imaginary, but actually a boy that had lived in the apartment before us and had passed away.

Then, one early morning, I was in the kitchen preparing breakfast and lunch for my husband to take to work, when I saw the top of a boy's head with straight blond hair walking on the other side of the kitchen island. I walked to the side of the island and got on my knees, waiting for my son to come to me and hug me. But my son never came. I checked the bedroom and my son was asleep. I later realised that he was too short for me to have seen him over the island and that his hair was not that blonde.

If you asked my son where his friend was he would run and look around for him and call his name until he found him, and then he would bring him to you and say 'here he is'. My husband also once felt someone touching his head. We began to realise that perhaps Rolly was not imaginary, but a boy that my son was actually playing with, talking to and seeing.

The good thing about this is that Rolly never hurt my son or us. The scary thing was that he was not only at the apartment, but would go with us wherever my son went. After we moved back home, Rolly came home with us for a while and then just disappeared.

MY FRIEND WITH NO NAME

Ever since I can remember I have always had visits from a little girl, though I have never told anyone before now. She has long black hair, wears a white night gown and her eyes are just eyeballs. No pupil or anything. And everything else seems normal about her, except for many cuts and bruises. One time she appeared to me looking a little different: no cuts or bruises and with blonde hair and full eyes. On that occasion she did not scare me at all. But this was an exception.

I would hear her talk to me. Sometimes she gave me right advice and other times she gave me wrong advice. She would tell me that I should not do this and I should do that. For example, if ever I was mad at someone she would tell me to forgive them, whereas other times, if ever I saw someone being teased or picked on she would tell me to go pick on them too, in her childlike manner.

There were days she would actually enter into me and make me talk aloud. I never felt cold, or scared or anything. If I am honest there was absolutely no emotion in me whatsoever. Everything just went blank, other than whatever she was making me say. There are other times I would actually have conversations with her.

She has been with me from the moment I could walk all the way up to now and I am 19 years old. I have had dreams about her, I have had nightmares about her and I have seen her face in some of my pictures before. I would put them on the computer and edit them out because I did not want anyone to be scared of me when they saw them.

As I began to grow up she became a bit more of a blur, only visiting me every once in a while. To this day I still sometimes hear her voice, but after growing up with her she does not frighten me. She has always been kind of my friend, even though she has never told me her name. Still, I love her and if she ever left me completely I would be lost and very lonely, no matter how many people I have in life.

I LOVE LUCY

When I was around the age of eight, I remember that I used to talk to a little girl. I lived with my grandma and my mum in Mansfield Woodhouse. My mum just brushed it off as me having an imaginary friend, but to me she was very real.

The little girl had light brown hair that she always wore in pigtails and had green eyes. She told me her name was Lucy. She told me that she was 11 years old and that this was her home. I told my mum and my grandma everything Lucy told me. Lucy was possessive. When my mum would call me for dinner or something, she would beg me not to leave. I always told her that I had to go, but later she would be really annoyed at me. She would throw toys at me, pinch me and hit me. Once, she even pulled my hair so hard that she pull a fistful of blonde hair out. The first time my mum became worried was when she found a bruise Lucy had given me.

Approaching my ninth birthday, I remember taking a bath. Lucy was mad that day. I cannot remember what I had done to make her so angry. She came in the bathroom and dunked my head under the water. I could not breathe, so I splashed and kicked my feet, and eventually my grandma came in to see what was wrong. She tried to pull me up, but Lucy was still pushing me down. My grandma called for my mum, and Lucy had became so aggravated by then that she let out sort of this horrible screech and cry.

My mother called for a priest the next day. I cannot remember much of that day. I sort of erased it from my memory. What I do remember is that right before the priest was about to wash down the house with holy water, I heard this little giggle in my ear. It was Lucy. She whispered, 'Goodbye, Stacey. It was really fun playing with you. I'll miss you.'

IT'S MY PARTY!

When my son was young, maybe three years old, he had an imaginary friend named Jenny. He would play with her all the time. He said when he was not playing with her she lived with God. We asked why she lived with God and he said it was because she had died in a fire. We are not a church-going family, so the fact he would say that was just odd. She apparently played with him for many months.

One week he kept talking about how it was going to be Jenny's birthday soon. Then the news came from Tommy that tomorrow was Jenny's birthday and we should go for a walk in Wollaton Park and then have a party, maybe even get a cake.

The next day we went to the park, then had a party. We bought a little cake for his imaginary friend and then waited for Jenny to come. But she never visited my son that day or ever again.

He cried a lot, as he was devastated she did not come to the party. Because we thought she was imaginary we tried to convince him that she was there and that we should have the cake anyway, but that only made him cry more because he said she was not imaginary; she was real to him and he could not see her there.

HOME IS WHERE THE HEART IS

This happened when I was a small boy. I think the year would have been about 1964 as we had just moved to Mansfield.

Our house was very big. As soon as we walked into that house I ran into the cupboard under the stairs, and ever since I would stay under there for hours. One night at dinner, my mother asked me why I stayed in the cupboard so much. I told her I was playing with a boy. She asked me what the boy's name was I told her I did not know but I would find out.

The next day I ran into the kitchen yelling, 'I know his name, I know his name!' I told her I only knew his last name. My mum was so curious, convinced by how real I found him, that she went to the library and looked up the name. She eventually found his name and that he had died of a fever in 1762. She also found out that he had a sister who was murdered over at her friend's house not long after her brother's death.

One night we were at a party next door. A man came down to get some ice. When he had got the ice he turned around and saw me, a boy in a buttoned shirt and a girl in a silk white dress with black hair and a red bow. The man dropped the ice and ran.

One night we were heading up to Newark for Christmas at my grandma's house. When my mum tried to shut the car door I started screaming 'he's coming, don't shut the door', so when he was in, she shut the door. When we got there that night we were all sitting around the fire when my Aunt Judy asked, 'So Clive, how is your imaginary friend?'

'He's fine, actually he's here tonight. See, his hand is on your leg,' I said. For the rest of the night we sat there and looked at the boy that everyone thought only I could see.

CASPER THE GHOST

When I was 13 years old my aunt bought a grandfather clock for her girlfriend, and the day she bought it my 'imaginary' friend Casper showed up. I named him 'Casper' after the cartoon film character, as it seemed pretty apt. He was seven years old, had straw-blonde hair, wore denim overalls, a white T-shirt and red shoes. He changed the channels on the TV to cartoons for me and banged the cupboard doors when the cats were hungry. He scared my aunt, grandma, dad and mother – everyone, in fact, except me.

I giggled at his antics and loved to play with him. Then one day my aunt brought in a medium. Without telling the woman that I saw him and what he looked like she described him perfectly.

Then, a month later my aunt's girlfriend moved out as they had split up and she took the clock with her. Casper left with the clock.

Still, 10 years later, I will be with my friends out walking around and then I will see an old lady or a little kid and stop to say hello and my friends will ask who I was talking to, or I will look at them for a little while, grab my friend's attention and say, 'That old lady is really staring me out' and turn to look and the old lady will be gone.

I am no longer scared by it all. I do not go to church, and I am not really religious. In fact, the most religious thing I have done is wear a wooden cross on an old string. I see demons sometimes walking down Maid Marion Way or standing in front of the lions in the market square, things that would terrify anyone but I face them and smile then turn away. They do not scare you much when you see them everyday.

CHAPTER 12
DIVINE INTERVENTION

Divine intervention is a term used when a spiritual or unexplained power appears to have had a hand in changing an outcome, usually giving protection in some way to the person concerned.

A lot of people believe in fate, and in this chapter it could be argued that although the odds were stacked against the person involved, it simply was not their fate or karmic path to proceed in the situation, so an outside force changed the outcome.

SAVED BY AN ANGEL

In 1979 I had a horrible experience when I was a student in Nottingham. I had always been interested in the occult, but as I got older I stopped being obsessed with the paranormal and tried to live my life without it.

One evening my best friend, Paul, brought his daughter's ex-boyfriend Daniel over to my house. We all went out for a drink in the city and I thought Daniel was really sweet and felt so sorry for him that he had been dumped by Paul's daughter, Dawn.

Daniel told me later, back at my house, that he was into Wicca. For some strange reason as I stood in the hall with him, I thought I could hear whispering voices, but I knew he had not said anything and that Paul was in the lounge. I said to Daniel, 'Did you hear that?' He just looked at me startled as though I was not meant to hear and said 'Yes'.

He then had an odd sort of look on his face. My stomach turned and something did not feel right. I was scared by this and the voices, so I decided to go to bed and tell Paul about it in the morning. I went upstairs to get two quilts and two pillows for them to sleep downstairs.

As I left my bedroom loaded with bedding under both arms, I felt my footing miss the second step and I started to fall forwards from the top of my steep staircase. At the bottom of the stairs were numerous things including a bicycle against the wall and a rigid telephone table with a lamp on it. I knew, as I started to fall, that I was in trouble. I screamed. All of a sudden I had what felt like feathery wings wrap around me, and I passed out as I tried, but failed, to grab the banister rail.

The next thing I knew, after coming round seconds later, was that I was sitting on the second to bottom stair totally unharmed and still holding the bedding under both arms. Paul and Daniel came rushing in. Paul said he had expected to see me lying dead or badly hurt as he heard me scream. How had I defied gravity like that?

I later found out that Daniel had thought Paul and I were having an affair, and because he still loved Dawn he was totally against me as Dawn did not care for me much either. Was it dark powers at work here and then an angel catching me? I do not know. But I think I was meant to hear those voices that night as some kind of warning.

MY DAD THE GUARDIAN ANGEL

My dad passed away in May 2001 of a massive heart attack in his home in Newark, with my mother in the next room. It was quick and fast with no time for a goodbye. I have always believed in an afterlife and had discussed this with my father prior to his passing as he was afraid of what was to come.

I believe that our body is the vessel in which our soul or spirit resides. When we die our soul leaves the body and crosses over to the other side, another dimension. Nevertheless, I took his death very hard.

That night at my parents' home I went out and looked at the beautiful stars in the sky remembering what my dad always told his three grandchildren, 'When I am gone from you I will never really be gone. I will be the soft stars that shine at night, and the wind that blows through the trees, that will be me!'

I prayed for my dad to give me a sign that he made it and told him I would never say goodbye in my prayers, so long as I felt he would be near me and I would see him again. I have recieved many such signs over the years, the first being three feathers on my car door, many come in the form dragonflies and much more. But the best was the night he came to me and sat on my bed, holding my hands and telling me he was okay, at peace and free of pain. He looked just as he did before he passed, only better somehow. He told me I was right about what I thought and for me to go on with my life and he would be watching over me and we would be together again in time.

BLAST FROM THE PAST

In 1992 I was driving my car towards Kimberley. It was a clear day and I was approaching the turning to Watnall Road, when all of a sudden a van hit me from behind. The car jolted forward, and obviously I was in shock so I stopped the engine and got out of the car.

I was standing in the middle of the road, when two people approached me. They were dressed in 1950s style clothing and the lady had a felt hat on as they walked towards me arm in arm. They just looked like something out of a 1950s *Good Housekeeping* magazine. They stopped and asked me if I was OK, and I replied that I was fine, apart from being a little shaken. The couple then walked past me.

My curiosity got the better of me and I immediately turned to where they were walking, but the pair had disappeared into thin air. I could clearly see all the way down the road in all directions so there was no way that they could have run anywhere or walked into a driveway in the split second from when I turned round.

SPIRIT GUIDE

When she was between the ages of 13 and 17 year old, my daughter was a pupil at Hollygirt school in Nottingham and had to catch the bus to school from the centre of the Nottingham.

She used to tell me that every time she went outside, or waited for the bus, she would see the same man. He always wore a long brown mac, glasses and had long grey hair. She used to describe him as looking like 'a disciple'. Now, if he had just appeared when she was waiting for a bus, then you could call in coincidence, but no matter what time or what route of bus she took, the man was always standing at the side of her. She could not escape him; even if she went shopping as he would appear, walking at the side of her.

Obviously, at first the man's presence scared my daughter, but over the years she started to see him as some sort of comfort and felt safe when he was around. We strongly believe that he was some sort of guardian angel or spirit guide that was with her for protection.

NOT MY TIME

One day I was walking near the Trent Bridge Inn in Nottingham and wanted to cross the main road. I pressed the crossing button and started to walk when the green man was flashing. I walked across the first road and stood on the island in the middle, ready to cross the next. Again, when the green man started flashing, I proceeded to cross the road but all of a sudden I felt a pair of two big hands pick me up and spin me around, placing me back on the island, just as a car came speeding past, after jumping the lights.

I stood there in shock, looking all around me – there was nobody around, and I realised nothing physical could have saved me because I would have seen it. I was alone. Whatever it was, it saved my life as I would almost certainly have been hit by that speeding car.

CHAPTER 13
PAST LIFE

A past life experience is said to have occured when a living person is able to recall events, people and information about a time in the past, which they believe they have lived in.

In regression a person is often able to impart direct information about who they believe to have been in a previous life, without having any knowledge as to where or why they have given the information. This information is able to be researched and verified and often has no link whatsoever to their present life. Sometimes people believe that they are able to glance at their own past lives through dreams or in a meditative state.

It could be argued, however, that the information that they are seeing is merely a memory recall or an inherited memory, which is contained with the brain. Whatever the true explanation of past life experiences, it is an interesting tool, which can help you overcome present-day difficulties by viewing them as the 'third person'.

PAST LIFE MEMORIES

When I was three (as I was told by my mother, I was a little young to remember at the time) I used to often talk about missing my aunt. This was not out of the ordinary, however, as we had just moved, so naturally my mum thought that I was talking about my aunt who we had just moved away from. She dialled her number so I could talk to her, but I was very upset apparently because I did not want to talk to that aunt. Instead I wanted to talk to my aunt 'who I lived with when my parents died'. My mother was obviously shocked by what I was saying.

Later my grandmother called to see how we liked our new house and everything. My mother was worried about me so she told my grandma about this things I had been saying. My grandmother believes in past lives and thought I was speaking about one and told my mum to get as much out of me about it as she could.

Over the next week my mother only got out of me that my parents had died and I was sent to live with my aunt. I talked about living in Nottingham and that I rode a horse to school and that I had died at 17. I would not tell her any more.

After all that everything returned to normal. Well, up until the time I was eight, that is. It was the night before Easter and the house was quiet. My parents were downstairs but I was bored out of my mind so I was cleaning my room. I picked up all my clothes, then took some dirty dishes down to the kitchen.

On my way back to my room, I stopped to stroke my cat. I was two feet away from my room when I saw a hand come out of the door and knock down a picture that was hanging next to my door. It was the palest hand I ever saw and had long, thin fingers. I turned and feld down the stairs to my brother's room, screaming.

When we went back upstairs the picture was on the floor where the ghostly hand had left it. I never saw it again and, as before, everything was normal for a while after that. About a year ago, however, I started seeing different types of ghostly people walking around me, who said nothing and seemed not to appear to anyone else. I even had a few weird dreams. They stopped for four mouths and have starting again now. It is scary not knowing what's coming next!

DID I SEE MYSELF?

I was in the last year at University and lived in a rented room in Beeston. The house was big and old and was home to four other students. As I was the last one to move in, and had therefore been allocated the smallest room, which I did not mind too much as it was the brightest room in the house and the sun would shine through the large window in there and fill up the space.

One day I decided to put up some hanging crystals at the window, to make the most of the light shining through. They were lovely, as when the sun shone through them they placed little rainbows all over the walls.

On one particular day, I was getting ready to go to my lecture, when I noticed that there were a lot more rainbows than usual. I did not think too much of it, putting it down to the fact that the sun must have been in a different position. I walked over to the mirror to brush my hair but when I looked into it, I did not see my own reflection but a reflection of a little girl wearing Victorian clothing. I could see all her details and then, no sooner had I taken it in, she disappeared before my eyes and my own reflection was where it should have been all along. Had I been the little girl in one of my past lives?

CHAPTER 14
UFOS

Many people believe that a UFO is a visitation from another planet or dimension, visiting our planet. However, it should be noted that a lot of sighting can be attributed to secret military missions, weather balloons or freak events of nature.

THE DRAYCOTT UFO

I worked at Parry's in Draycott near the border of Derbyshire and Nottinghamshire, and it was 1987 when my paranormal experience took place.

I had just finished work and I came out to my car to find that the windscreen had frosted over, and so I started to scrape off the ice.

I stood there cursing the fact that I was frozen solid and wanted to get home, when all of a sudden I saw a huge UFO fly over the top of the clock tower of the factory. It made no sound and seemed to glide through the air. The thing was huge and it made all the hairs on the back of my neck stand on end. Just behind it there was a red light, which seemed to follow it. There was no way that this was any normal aircraft.

I stood there watching it until it disappeared and then drove home in silence, not really understanding what I had just witnessed. To be honest I questioned my sanity, until the next day on the front page of the *Nottingham Evening Post* they were running a story from witnesses that had seen the UFO at the same time as me, and my sanity was restored.